Fearless

Familiars

An Oracle Guidebook

J Edward Neill

All Art by J Edward Neill

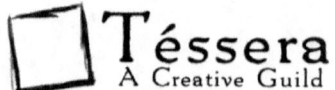

Téssera
A Creative Guild

Welcome to Fearless Familiar Oracle. This 52-card oracle deck includes all original art by artist J Edward Neill. The theme of Fearless Familiars? Black cats, all of whom represent a protective force in our lives.

Fearless Familiars is my third oracle deck. I paint a lot of felines, I mean a LOT, and so my focus this time is all the cats of earth, air, fire, and water whose spirits protect and enlighten us. Some people might look at a cat and see simply another beast. But with a keen eye, a wise observer will see creatures with whom we humans share a deep kinship. As goes their fate, so goes our own.

Herein you'll discover an array of haunting and intelligent felines. Each card embodies a single facet of protection, guardianship, and enlightenment. Reading deeper, and using your intuition, you'll discover the ways in which you protect yourself, sometimes for the better, and sometimes unnecessarily.

Fearless Familiars is an intuitive deck. The keywords and meanings for each card are but starting points. Please take the time to connect to each image in a meaningful way. For those who possess Haunted Cat Tarot, Fearless Familiars may be used in tandem with the tarot cards.

Always remember - this deck was made for you.

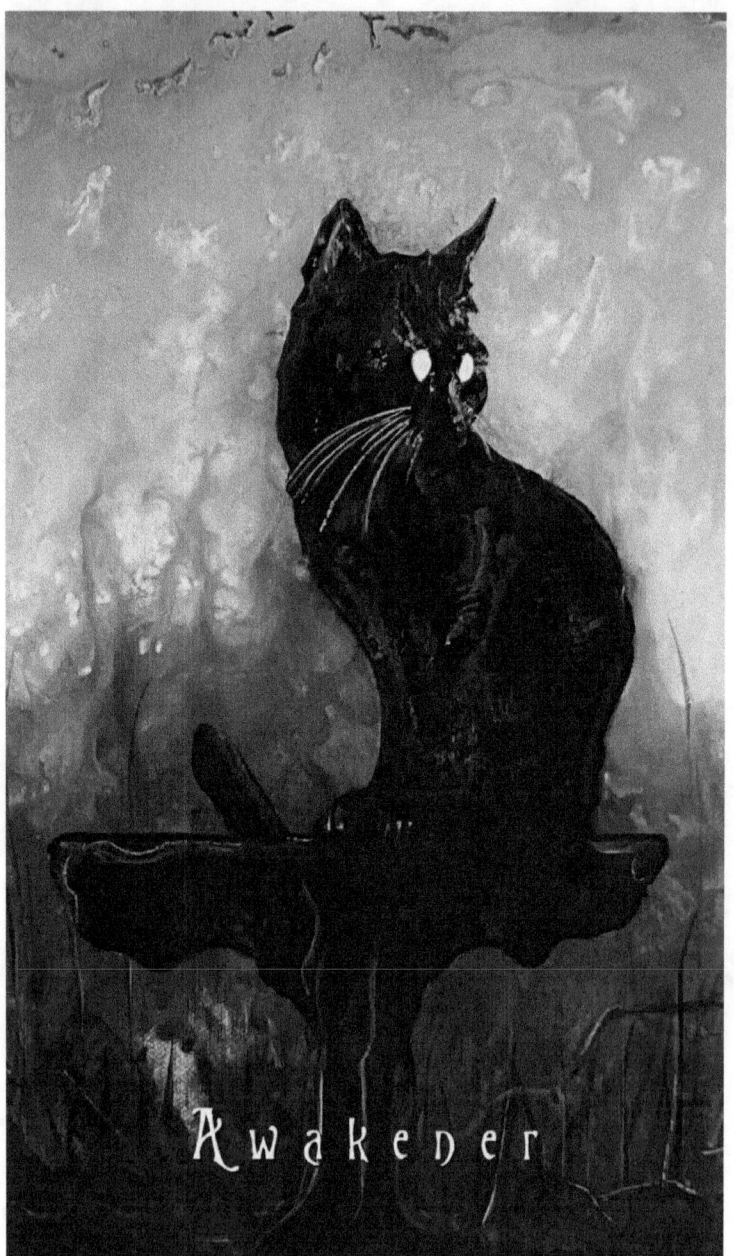

Awakener

Awakener

Keywords: Alertness, Knowledge, Alarm

If you've pulled the Awakener card, it could mean you're in for a big surprise. Perhaps you've just become aware of a new and exciting (or even risky) life situation. Or it could be that you've just learned something new and important, likely something about which you previously knew nothing. Whatever it is, it's significant to your near future.

The Awakener wants to bring you enlightenment. And although no knowledge is bad knowledge, it's what you do with it that counts. After the surprise wears off, you must decide.

Be awakened and wiser for it...

...or remain asleep.

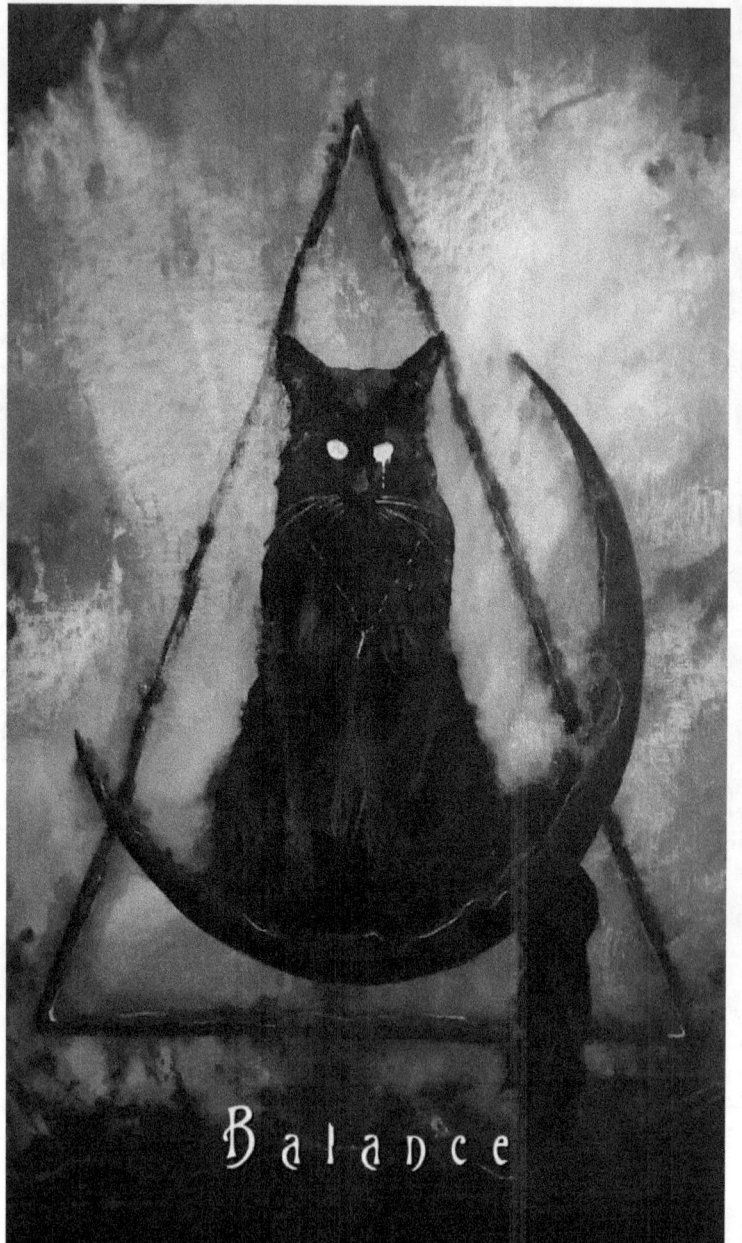

Balance

Balance

Keywords: Harmony, Equilibrium, Stability

The Balance familiar desires to keep you away from the perilous edges of life. If he's arrived in your card spread, it's a sign that you may be nearing the precipice of something important.

A big decision.

A take it or leave it opportunity.

A new job, relationship, or living situation.

When you see Balance in your hand, remember that it's possible to make big changes in your life without losing your sense of self. Stay true to you. Remember to consume all things in moderation, not excess.

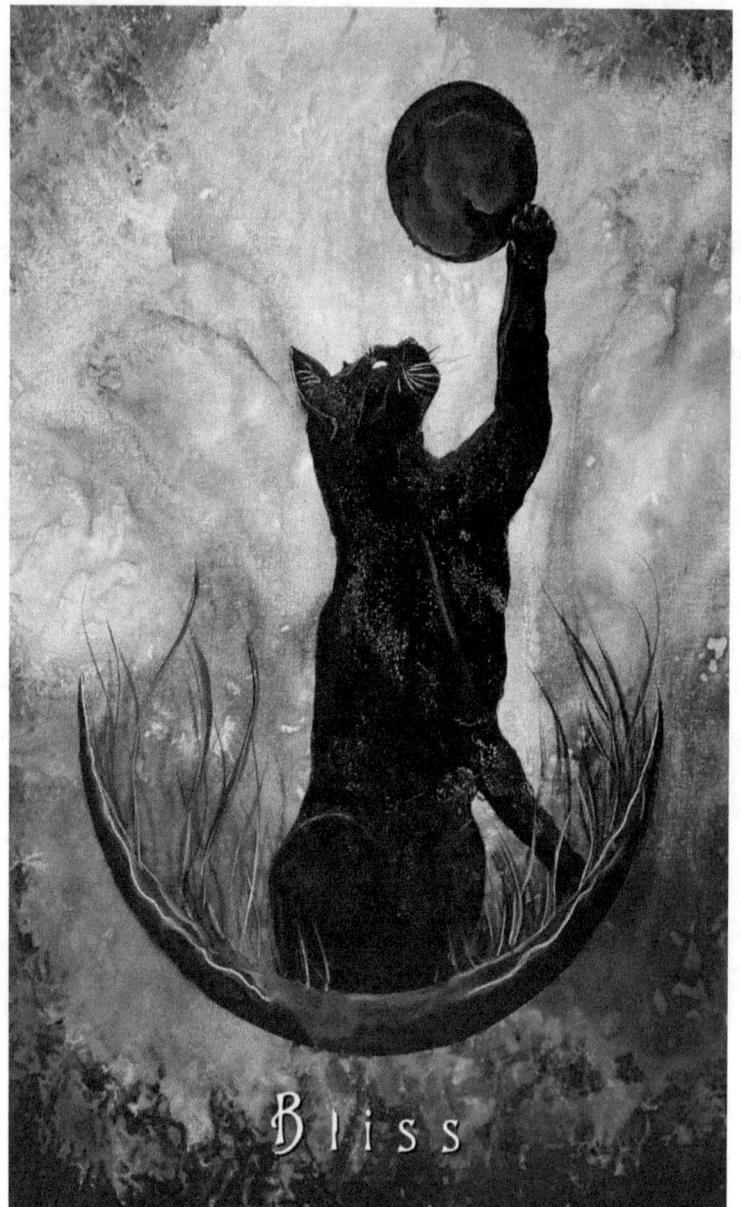

Bliss

Bliss

Keywords: Pleasure, Joy, Naivety

Ignorance is bliss, right?

If you've encountered the Bliss familiar, perhaps now is the time to sit back and savor a happy moment in your life. Let nothing ruin your fun. Send all naysayers back from whence they came.

It may be that you've recently reached (or are about to reach) a pleasant goal. Or perhaps you've discovered a new hobby or leisure activity. Or it might be that you're simply having a bit more fun than usual. In any case, consider allowing yourself to cherish the moment. They can be fleeting, these happy times, and over before you know it.

Bliss reminds us that sometimes the simplest shield against anxiety or worry is to enjoy what you already have.

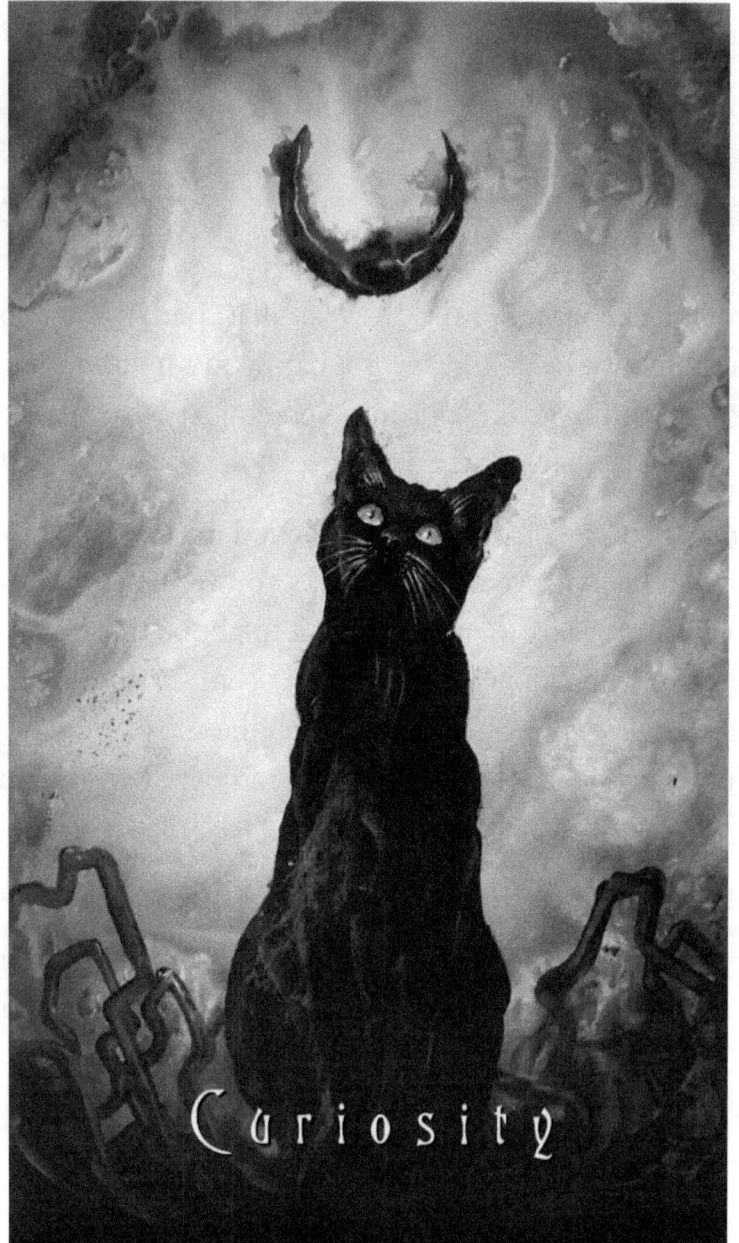

Curiosity

Curiosity

Keywords: Questions, Newness, Seeking

Curiosity killed the cat?

Maybe not.

One of the best ways to protect ourselves in this sticky thing we call life is to arm ourselves with *knowledge*. And one of the best ways to acquire knowledge is to seek it out. If you've pulled Curiosity, it might be time to sniff out a hidden truth.

Feel like someone's hiding something from you?

Be curious.

Need to know what really going on?

Dig deeper.

In any case, never stop being curious. It could make all the difference between being prepared and being caught totally off your guard.

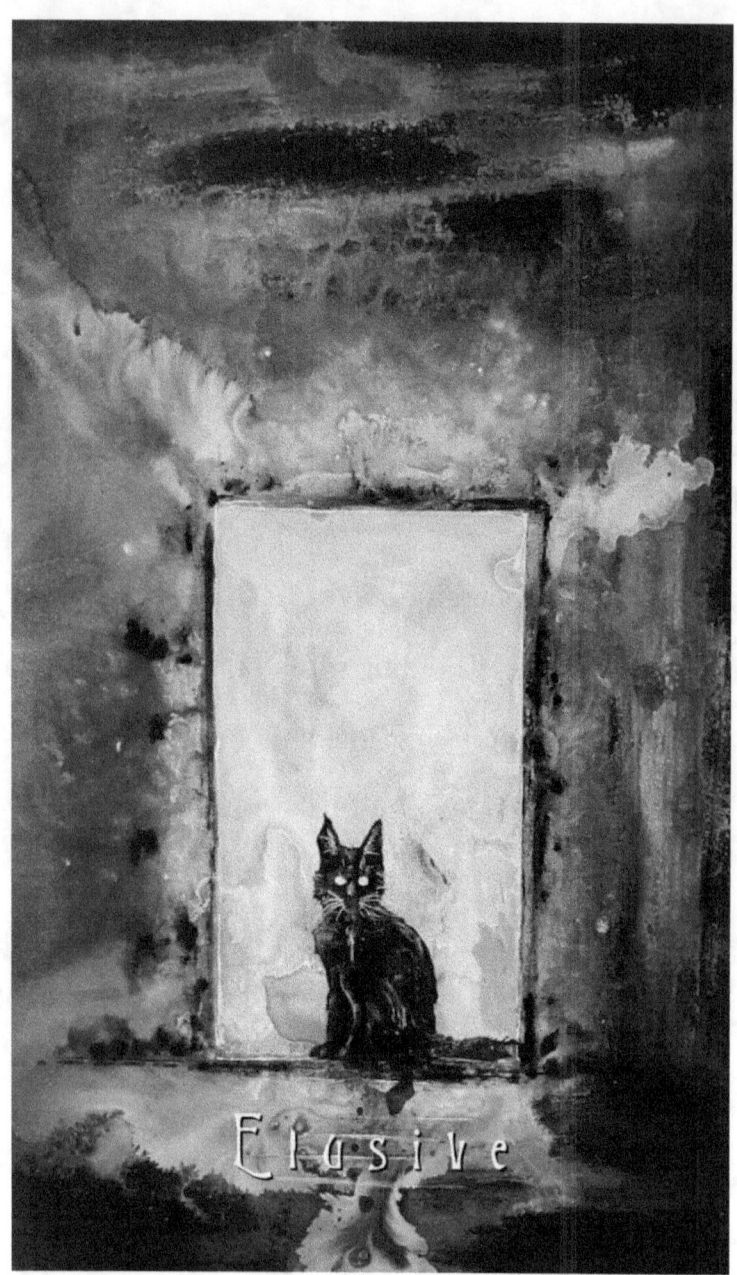

Elusive

Elusive

Keywords: Enigma, Mystery, Quickness

Some things are harder to catch than others.

If you've pulled the Elusive card, now might be the right time to stay extra light on your toes. After all, you don't owe it to the world to reveal everything about yourself or to be always accessible. It's okay to be mysterious at times, especially in new situations or when mingling with strangers.

Be nimble. Steer clear of trouble. Keep your head down until the storm passes. Remember to offer only as much of your heart and mind as you desire, and not one ounce more. While sometimes it's wise to meet life's problems head-on, this might not be one of those times.

The Elusive familiar reminds us to gauge new life situations carefully, and if needed, to leave them swiftly behind.

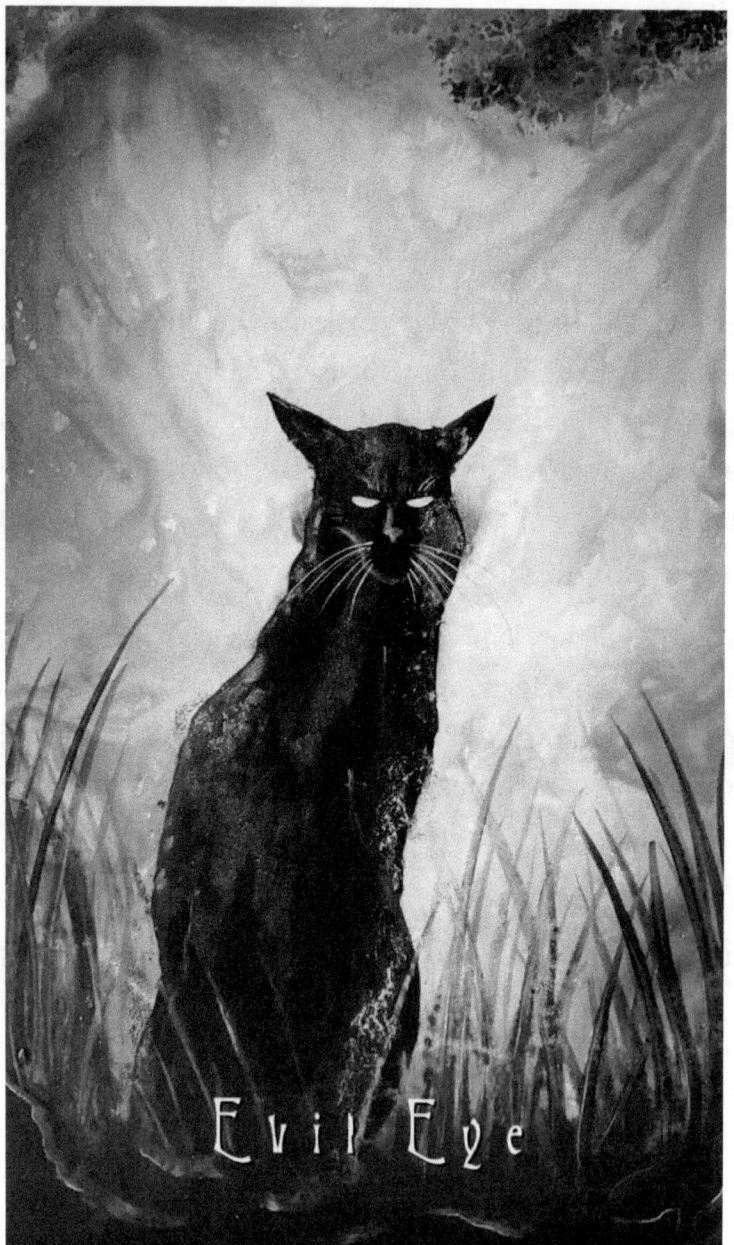

Evil Eye

Evil Eye

Keywords: Guarded, Wary, Distrust

We've all seen this look.

...in cats.

...in other people.

If you've pulled the Evil Eye, it might be that someone or something you don't quite trust has popped up in your life:

A sneaky coworker.

An unpleasant situation.

An ex-lover.

Whatever it is, it might be the right time for you to give this person or situation an evil eye of your own. Proceed with caution. Trust isn't always given freely, so make them earn it. And until they do, be on your guard.

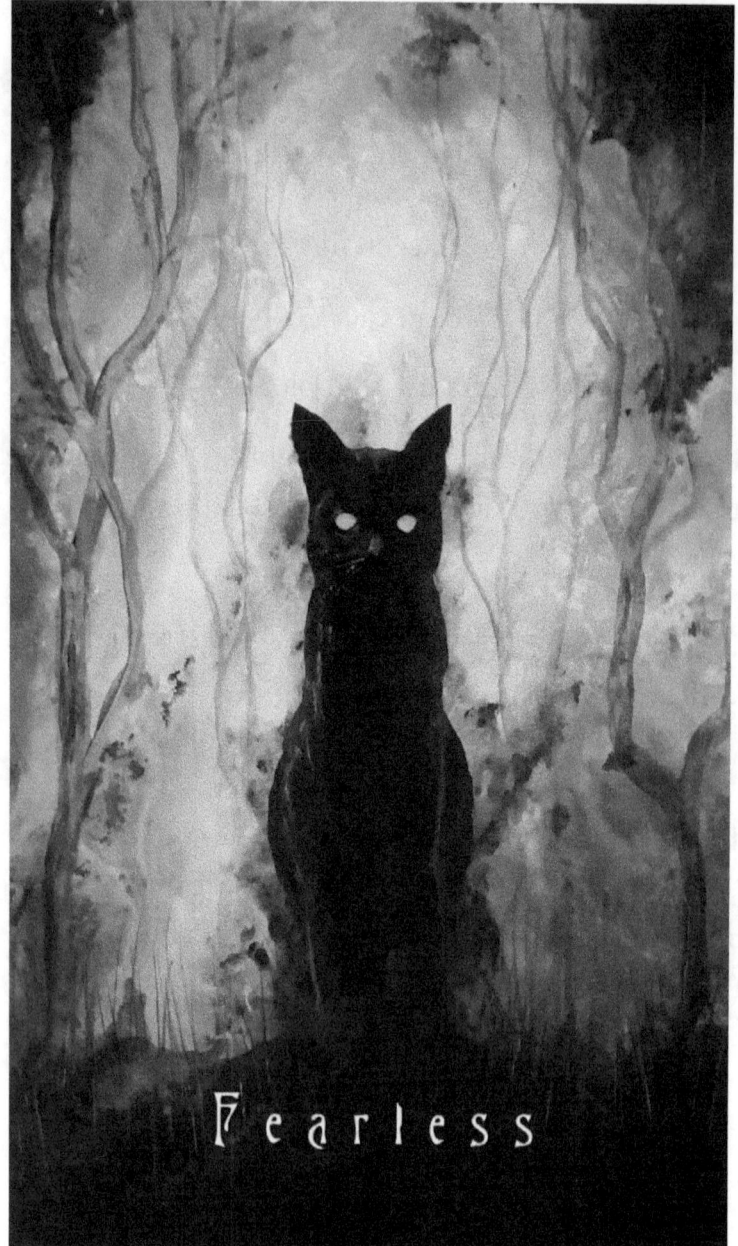

Fearless

Fearless

Keywords: Boldness, Bluntness, Confidence

Just as life sometimes calls for caution and trepidation, it just as often asks us to plunge into situations headlong. If you've pulled the Fearless familiar, today might be the day to shrug off your worries and anxieties. Ask for that promotion. Go on that date. Take what you want, and fear no repercussions.

Fortune favors the bold, or so they say. This isn't to suggest you embrace arrogance or overconfidence, but instead that you set aside words and wishes, and convert them to action.

The Fearless familiar wants you to chase down what you desire.

What are you waiting for?

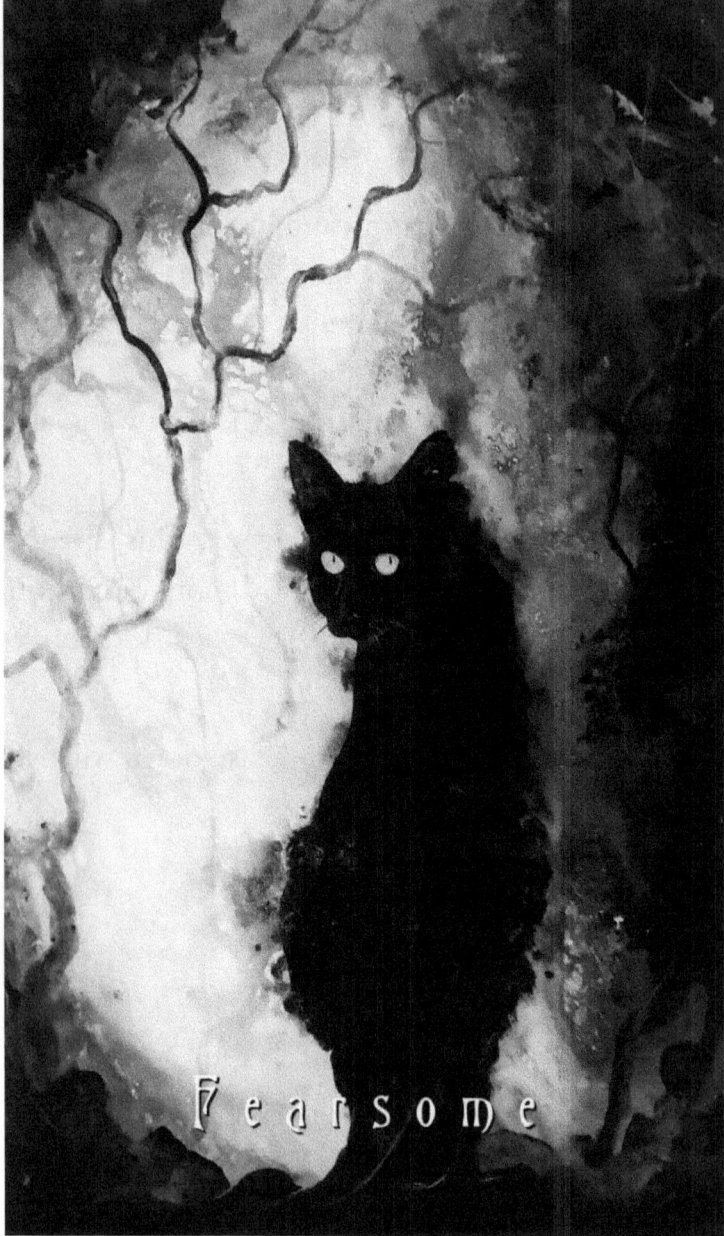

Fearsome

Fearsome

Keywords: Power, Control, Mastery

Not to be confused with the Fearless card, the Fearsome familiar desires that you become a force with which to be reckoned.

Thriving in this world means contending with people, places, and things that all seek to distract, coerce, or manipulate us. The best method of avoiding these fates? Rise above them.

If you've pulled the Fearsome card, now is perhaps the right time to adopt a more formidable posture. It may mean that you need to assume a leadership role at work or home. It may suggest that you stop allowing others to dictate the pace of your life, and to seize control of your own destiny. At the risk of appearing brash, maybe even ruthless, you should consider standing a little taller, puffing out your chest, and suffering no one to undermine you.

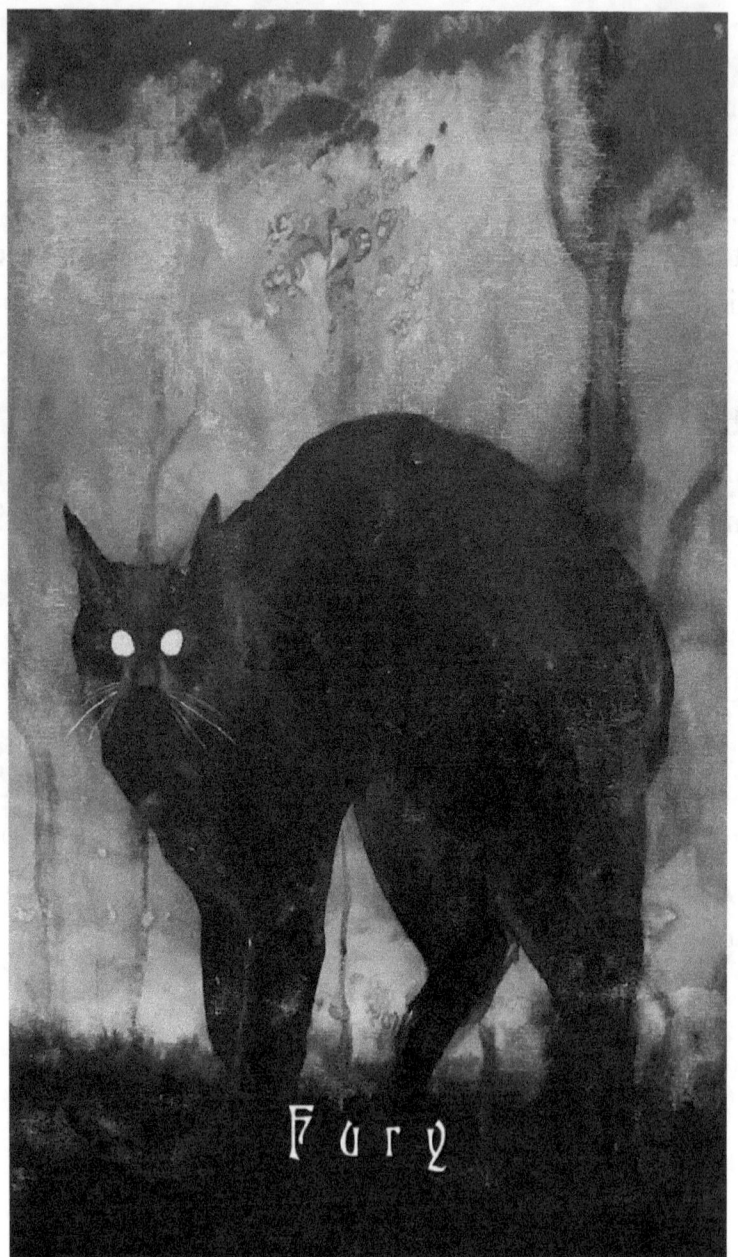

Fury

Fury

Keywords: Anger, Righteousness, Emotion

If the Fury familiar has arrived in your card spread, you might be experiencing powerful emotions. An injustice may have occurred in your life, and now there must be a reckoning.

Now...this isn't to say that the Fury card desires you to unleash your rage while wading, unrestrained, through a battlefield of your enemies.

But...

It could be time to vent. To focus on your powerful emotions and decide what needs to happen. To take raw feeling and shape it into meaningful purpose.

Fury reminds us that life's most important moments, good or bad, are accompanied by strong emotions. And while sometimes it's wise to hold those emotions at bay, at other times the only course is to embrace them, feel them deeply, and let those who matter know *exactly* what your heart is experiencing.

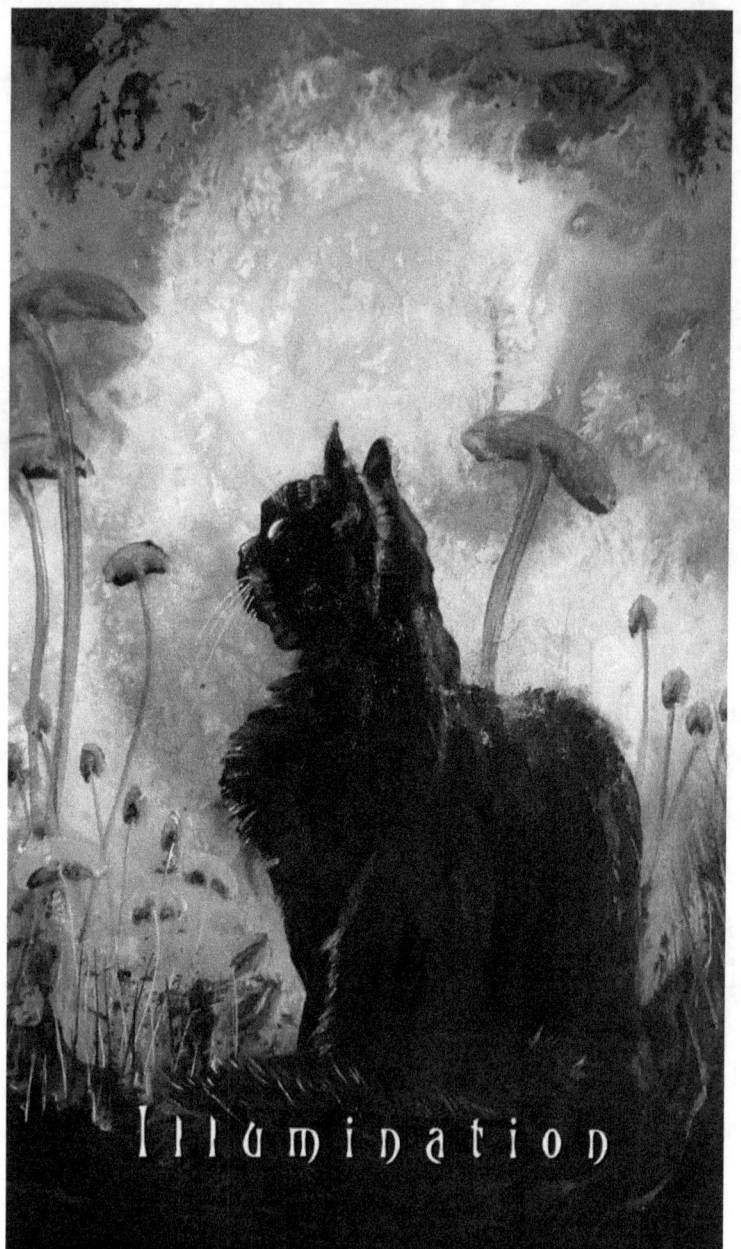

Illumination

Illumination

Keywords: Enlightenment, Clarity, Vision

When Illumination is pulled, it usually portends that some key facet in your life is about to shined upon by the light of truth. Like sunshine brightening a once cloudy day, things will soon come into focus. Blurry thoughts and feelings will become sharp. If doubt and uncertainty were fogging your mind, everything will now be clearer.

The Illumination familiar urges you to gaze skyward. It wants you to pry yourself from the mundane, domestic, and repetitive motions of your life, and to open your eyes to what lies above and beyond. For at least a little while, escape the doldrums and be filled with fresh hope.

Now is the time of new ideas, strong motivation, and renewed goals. Opportunity is close at hand.

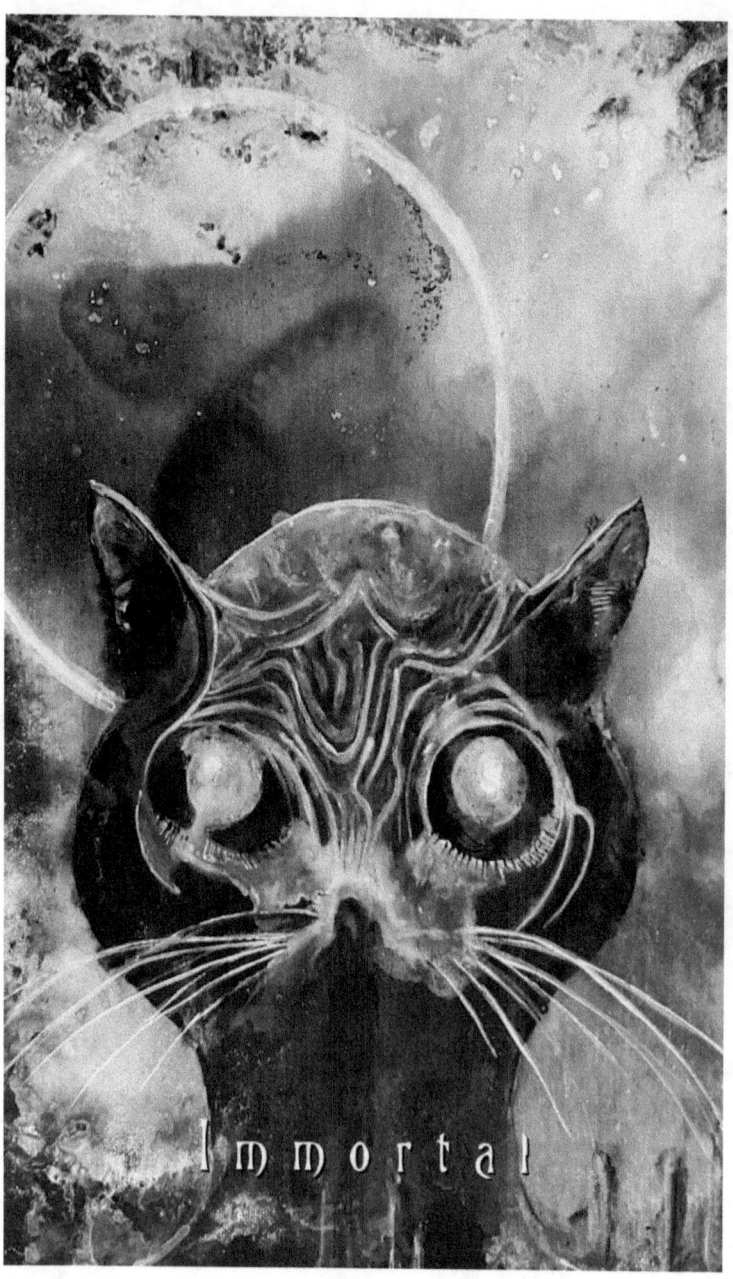

Immortal

Immortal

Keywords: Indestructible, Untouchable, Soul

Though your body may ache and your mind grow fatigued, in the end you above these things.

This is the message the Immortal familiar wants to bring you. Perhaps you fear sickness, exhaustion, or growing older. It might be that a nagging fear of death is on your mind, either for yourself or a loved one.

If you've pulled the Immortal card, it's likely because now is the time to see beyond the material. Money, possessions, and even people are temporary things. The only enduring power in this universe is your inner self, your *soul*. Nothing and no one can destroy this essential part of you. Remember this, and you truly are immortal.

The Immortal familiar reminds us that while fear and worry are natural things to feel, we should never let it become the largest part of ourselves. We are eternal, after all.

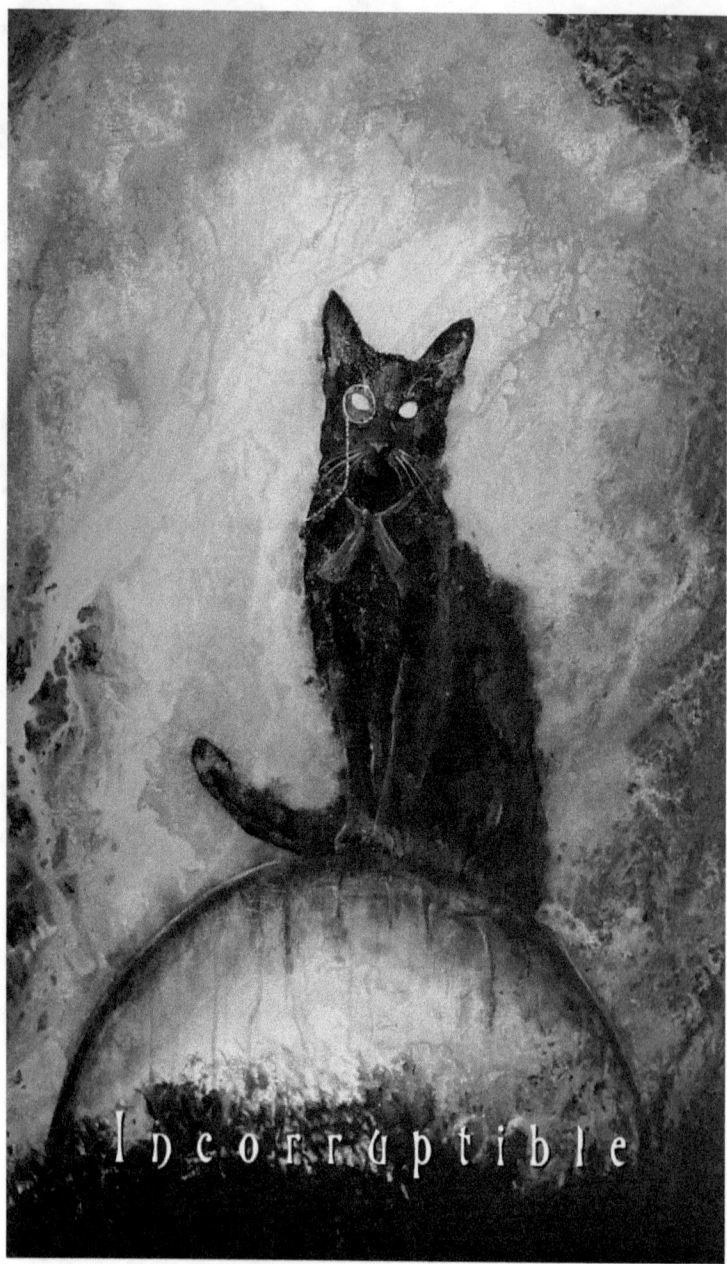

Incorruptible

Incorruptible

Keywords: Integrity, Honesty, Endurance

When the Incorruptible card arrives, it may be that your strength of character is about to be tested. Temptation awaits you, and you could be pulled toward actions that misalign with who you really are.

This is your reminder to endure. Whether temptation arrives in the form of another person, the allure of money, or an old vice rearing its head, you have the power to reject things you don't need in your life. Alternatively, if you do decide to give in, do so with a clear head and for reasons that will serve you in the long-term. In other words, don't compromise yourself for temporary gains.

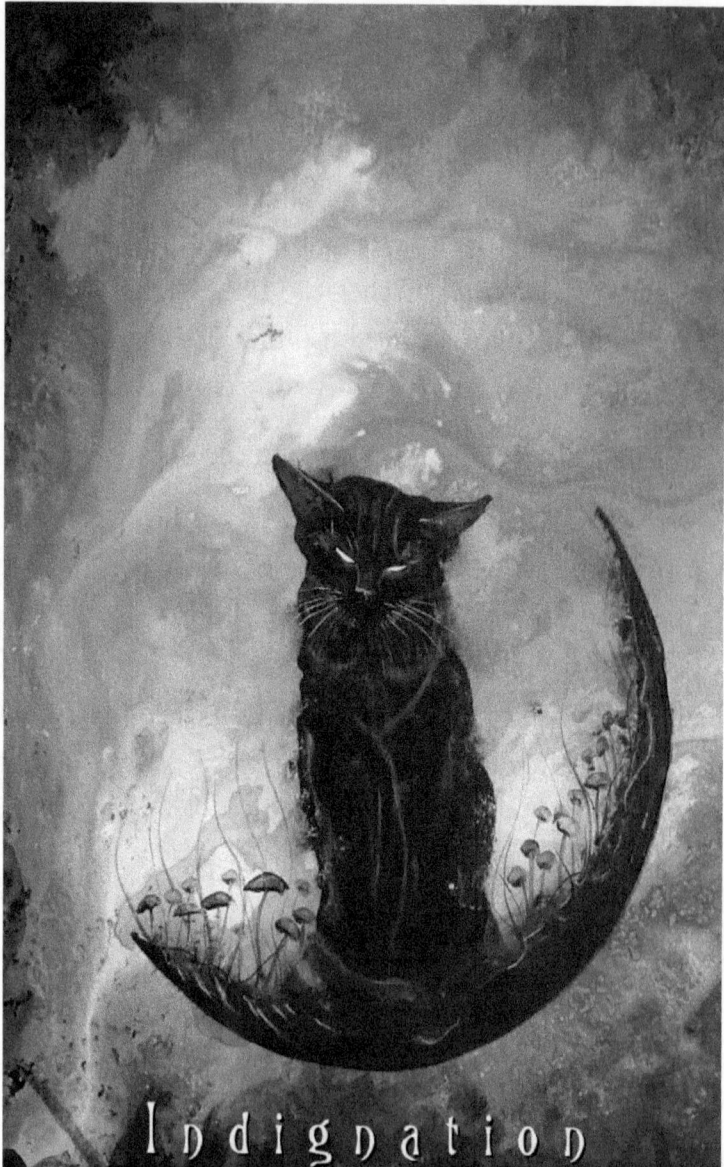

Indignation

Indignation

Keywords: Disgust, Humiliation, Resentment

If the Indignation familiar is pulled, you may feel as though someone or something has affronted you. Perhaps you've suffered some humiliation, or it might be that you've uncovered an unhappy truth which displeases you. It's a normal response, after all, to turn your nose away from unpleasant things.

If you've taken offense to something, it's wisest to gauge the intent. If you find yourself insulted or angry at something which wasn't intentional, it might be best to forgive and move forward. However, if offense was delivered to you on purpose, it's often prudent to remove yourself from the situation. Don't give the offenders what they want, which is typically a display of injured emotions.

Indignation reminds us that the feelings of disgust or emotional injury are useful if remembered and applied to the future, but damaging if they lead to lingering pain and suffering.

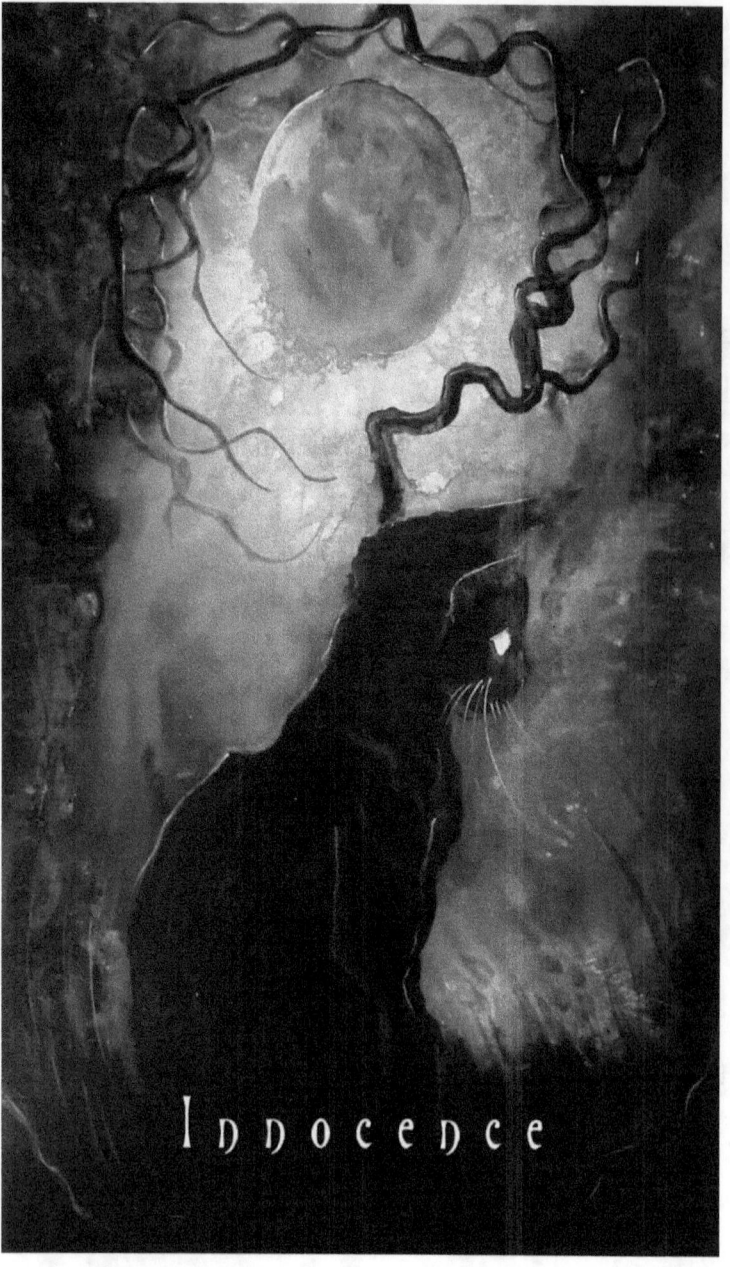

Innocence

Innocence

Keywords: Newness, Youth, Virtue

The youngest and most pleasantly naïve of all familiars, Innocence is here to teach and guide you. When it arrives in a card spread, it could mean a desire to return to simpler times, and to get back in touch with childhood experiences. Alternatively, it may be that you've found yourself in a new and possibly intimidating situation, such as a new job, relationship, or living space. Your innocence might be revealed, and it may be uncomfortable.

Innocence reminds us that it's completely acceptable to be a novice, and also understandable to desire a return to a younger, un-jaded state of mind. There is no shame in being a new arrival and no apology owed for making rookie mistakes. We were all innocent once, and we possess the power and often the desire to be innocent again.

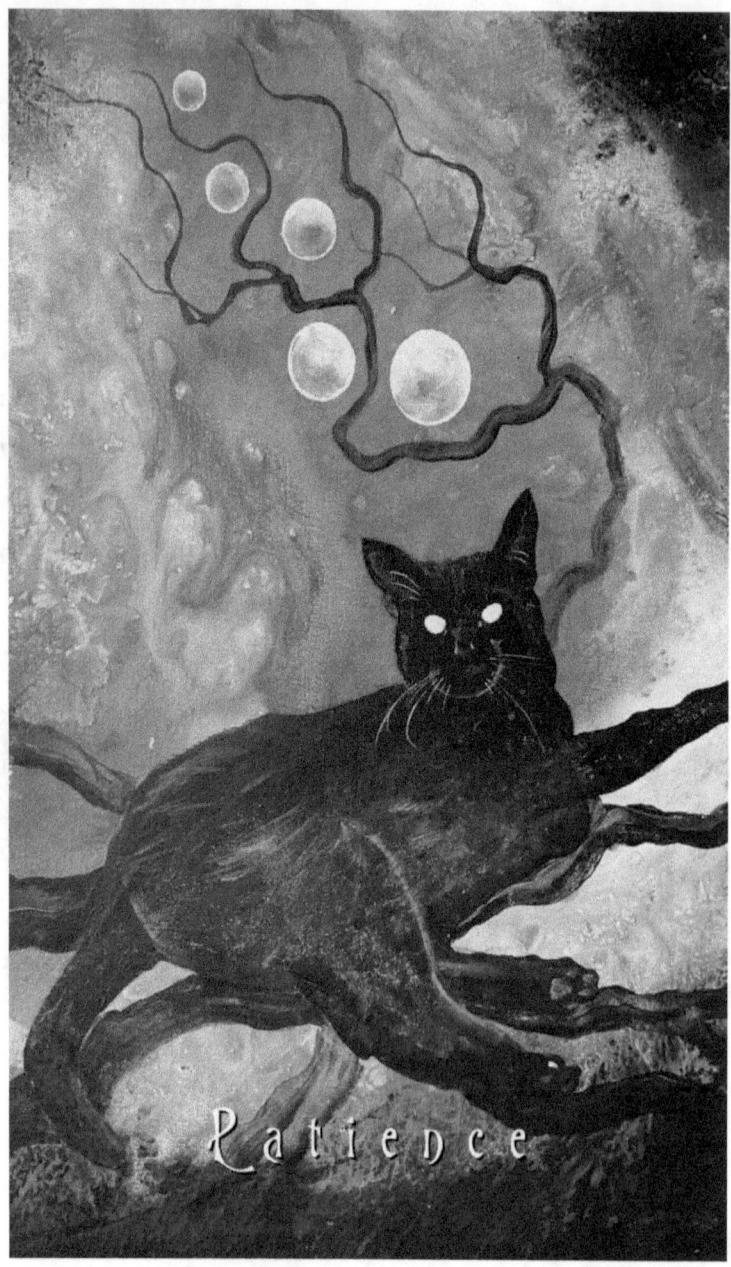

Patience

Patience

Keywords: Waiting, Persistence, Even-Temperedness

Slow and steady wins the race, or so they say.

If you've pulled the Patience card, it might be time to find yourself a comfy chair, because it could be a while before you get what you desire. A promotion at work, a new relationship, a question not yet answered—these things take time. Not everything in life accelerates at the rate we want.

On the other hand, it might be that you've started or are about to start a journey toward a brand-new goal, one that promises to consume plenty of time and energy. In this case, the Patience familiar wants you to take it step-by-step, day-by-day. Rushing things might earn you a subpar result. Playing the long game is the surest path to success.

Patience reminds us that the best things in life aren't free, they're earned. Be disciplined, and win the marathon.

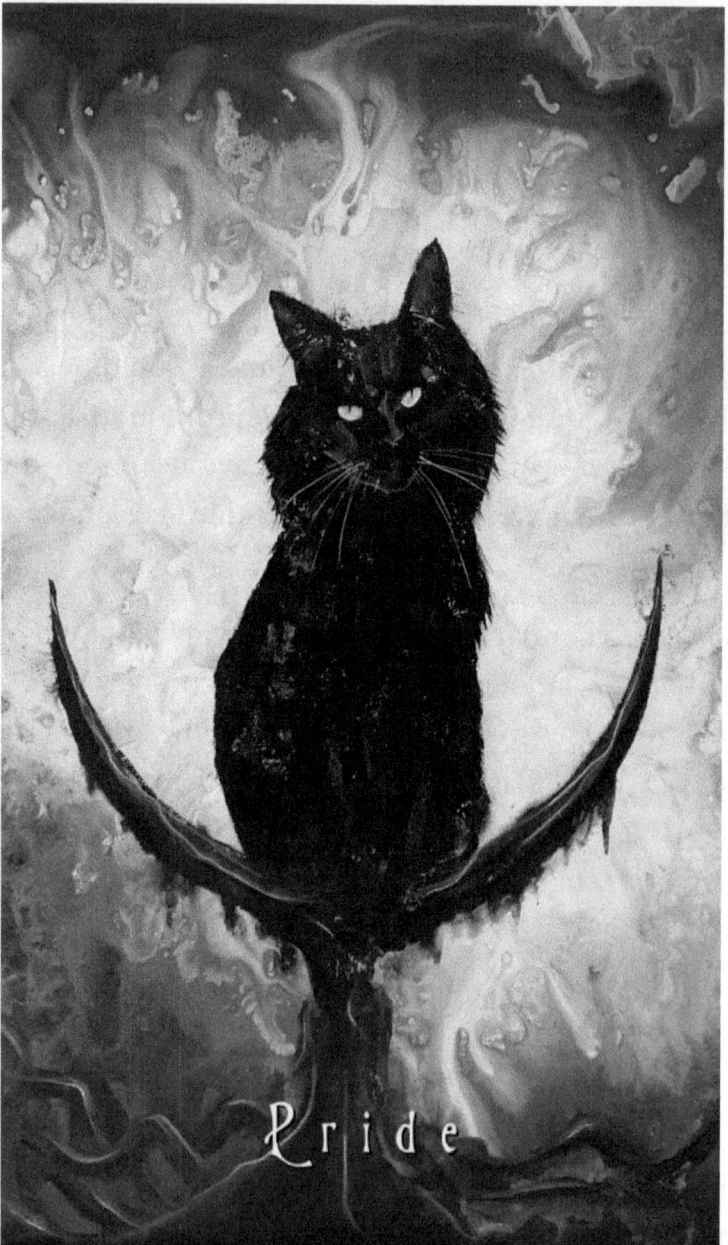

Pride

Pride

Keywords: Ego, Confidence, Self-Respect

'Pride before the fall,' so goes the saying. And yet, if you've pulled the Pride familiar, that's not the kind of pride in question here.

When this card appears, it's often because you've been presented with an opportunity to take a well-deserved bow for a recent accomplishment. Perhaps you've reached a goal or milestone in life, and you'd like to bask in the glow for a moment. Or maybe you've overcome some difficult hurdle, and feel as though it's worthy of self-praise.

The Pride familiar reminds us that there is strength in self-love, and that sometimes the best shield against negative emotions is a healthy dose of confidence. After all, feeling good about one's accomplishments isn't arrogance. Rather, it's an essential life skill in order to reach happiness.

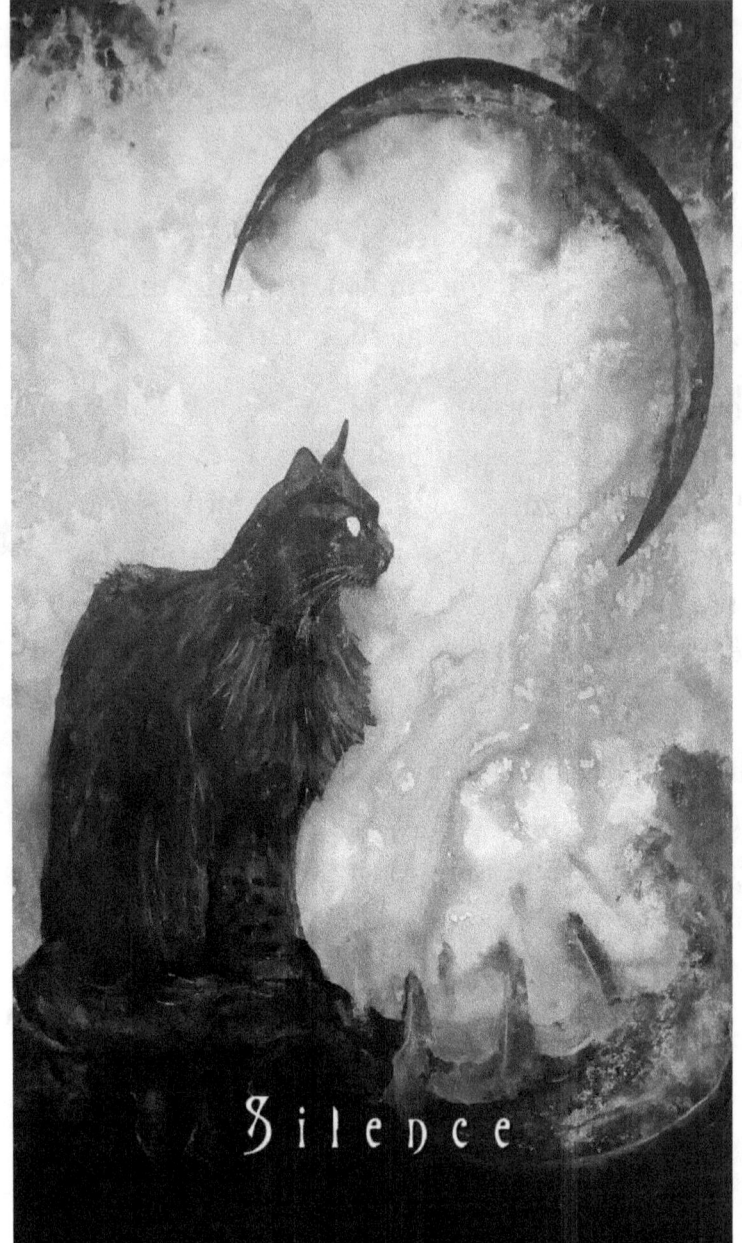

Silence

Silence

Keywords: Tranquility, Privacy, Peace of Mind

If you've encountered Silence, the pressure might be upon you to react to a person or situation. Whether at work or in your private life, someone or something may be pushing you for an answer. A feeling of immediacy could be weighing on you.

And yet...

Now is not the time for rashness, rushing in, or loudly spoken words. Sometimes, when prodded to action by a force which may not have your best interests in mind, your wisest recourse it not to react. It could be that saying and doing nothing in response to whatever or whoever pushes your buttons is not only a sound strategy, but could also lead to a better decision in the end.

Silence is a reminder not to let the world annoy you into motion. Reserve your actions for when they matter to *you.*

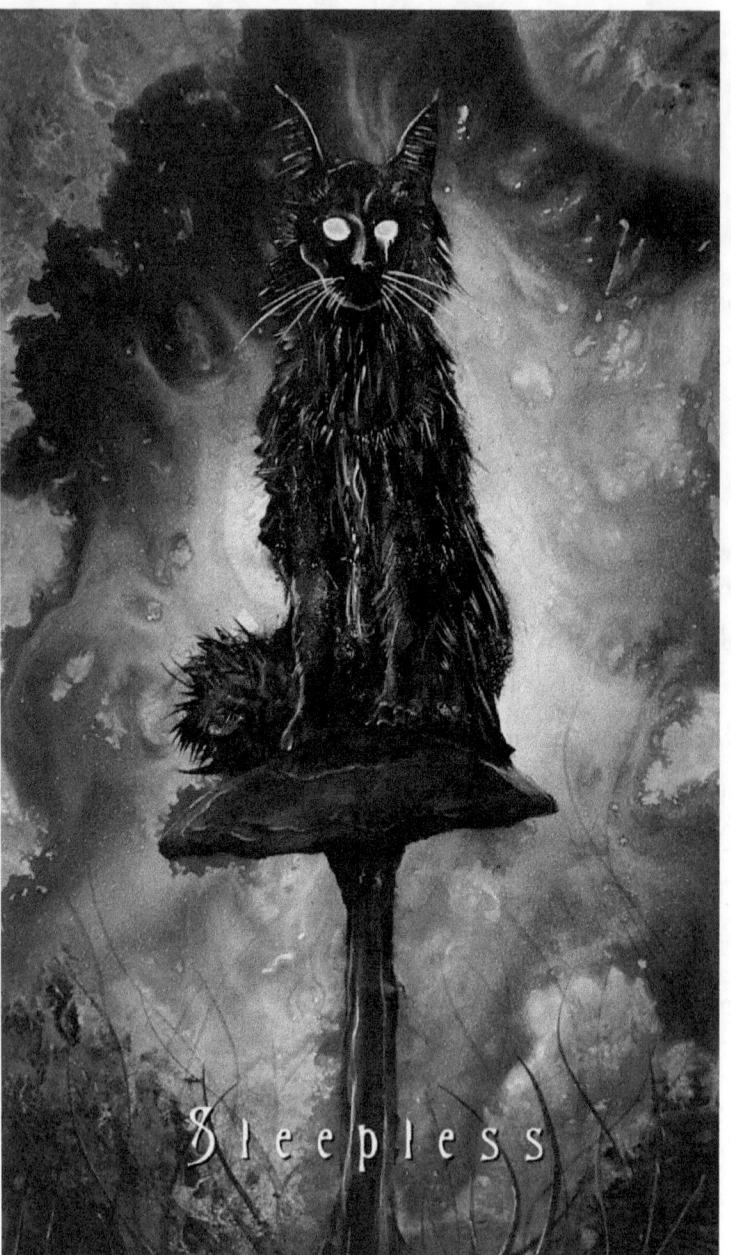

Sleepless

Sleepless

Keywords: Guarded, Awareness, Tension

The Sleepless familiar is here to keep a close eye on you. If you've pulled this card, the time to be on your guard is right now. It could be that a big opportunity is just around the corner, one you don't want to miss. Or it could portend trouble is on its way.

Sometimes, the best way to prepare for the future is to anticipate difficulty. That's not to say you should expect disaster, just that change seldom arrives without at least a dash of struggle. But if you're prepared for it, and if you're vigilant, your ship will sail all the smoother.

On the flip side, if difficulties are indeed inbound, you'll be best served not to be blindsided. It may cost you a few restless nights, yet it's far better to confront fresh challenges with a plan already in mind.

Sleepless reminds us to trust our intuition, and to exercise forethought whenever possible.

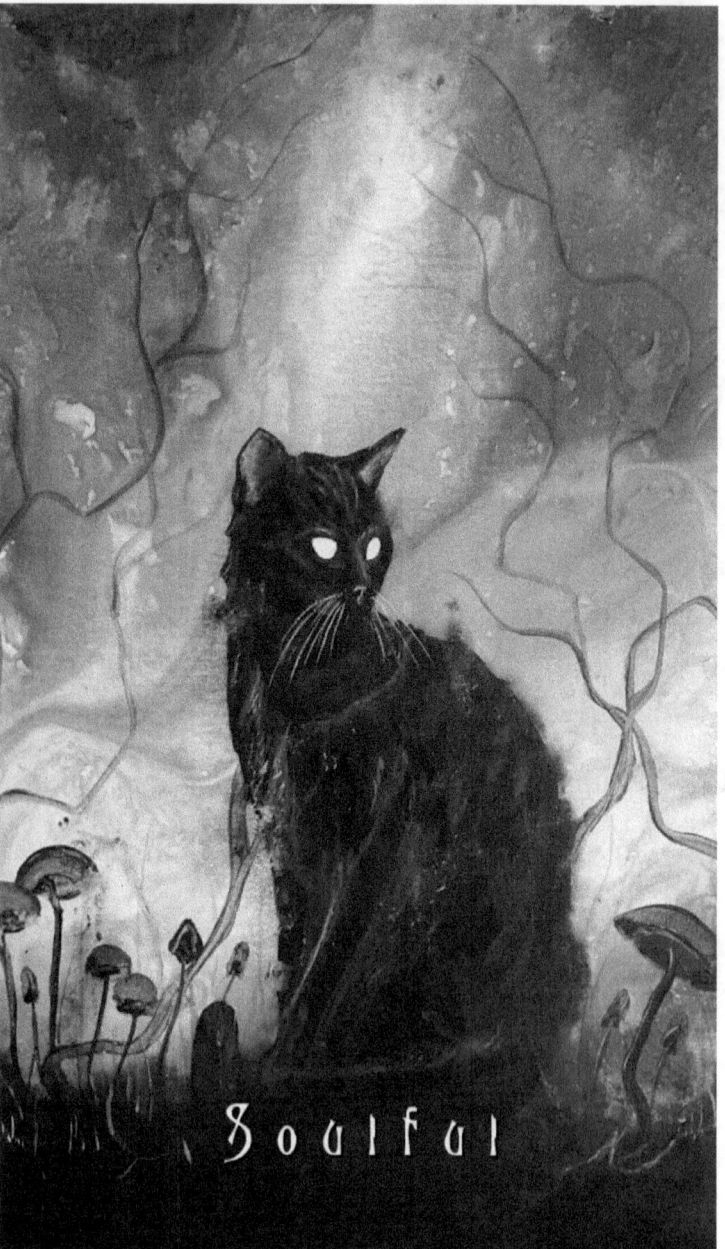

Soulful

Keywords: Conscience, Nurturing, Meaningful

When the Soulful familiar turns its gaze upon you, it's
likely time to consider the deeper meaning of life.
Whatever is happening to you right now, it's important
to dive below the surface of things to discover what's
really going on.

The Soulful card should invoke questions, such as:

Why is this really happening?

What do I truly desire the outcome to be?

Am I conscious of everyone's feelings in this matter?

What is the right thing to do?

Too often, we view things only from an outsider's
perspective. We see only the tip of the iceberg, and not
the depth and nuance of what lies deeper. The Soulful
familiar reminds us to look beyond the veil of everyday
existence to see what lies beyond.

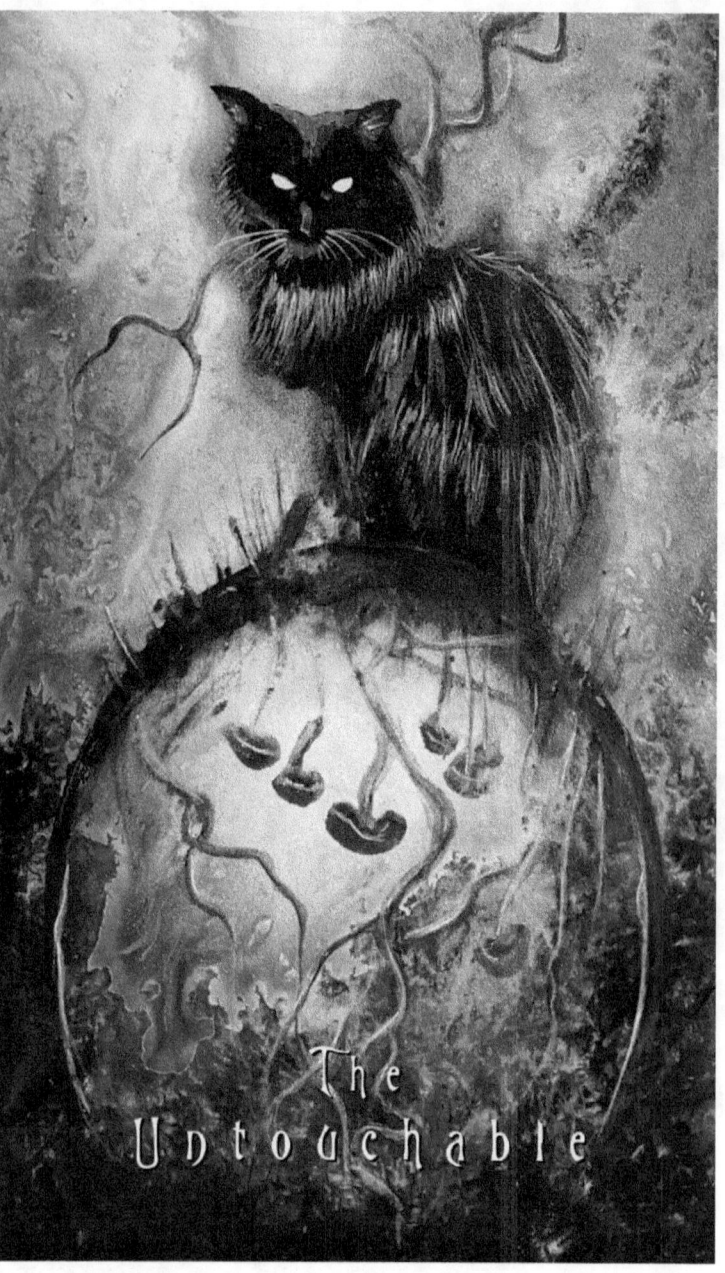

The
Untouchable

The Untouchable

Keywords: Hidden, Elevated, Immunity

There are times in our lives during which we must either rise above situations around us or remove ourselves from certain situations utterly and completely. If The Untouchable arrives in your card spread, now could be one of those times.

It could be that something is happening to you (or something you're actively pursuing) that is *beneath* you. Engaging in senseless debates, carrying on with detrimental relationships, working on goals without passion...these are examples of things The Untouchable wants you to exile from your life.

If this familiar could speak, it would say:

"You're better than this."

Right now, as in today, could be your best opportunity to climb higher than the things which drag you down. Remove yourself from negative things and remove negative things from yourself. Become untouchable.

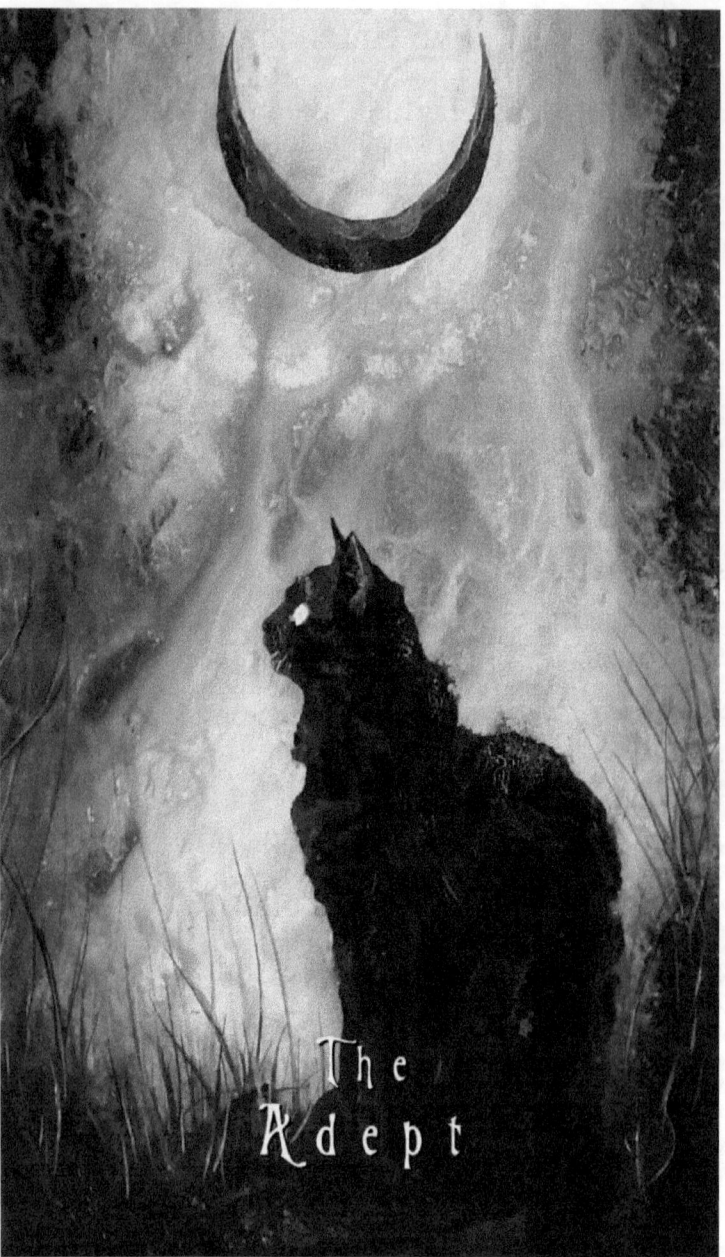

The
Adept

The Adept

Keywords: Skill, Deftness, Professional

When The Adept arrives, the moment is right to exercise your best talent.

It could be that you've shown restraint until now. Or maybe your confidence has wavered in the recent past. In any event, you should consider moving past any hesitation and bring to bear the full force of your skills.

Perhaps you're being challenged at work.

Or a purely physical obstacle is in your way.

Or an opportunity has arisen in your field of expertise.

The Adept wants to you to utilize your biggest strength, whatever it may be. You've put in the practice and honed your skills. You know you're good at this. Now it's time to show it.

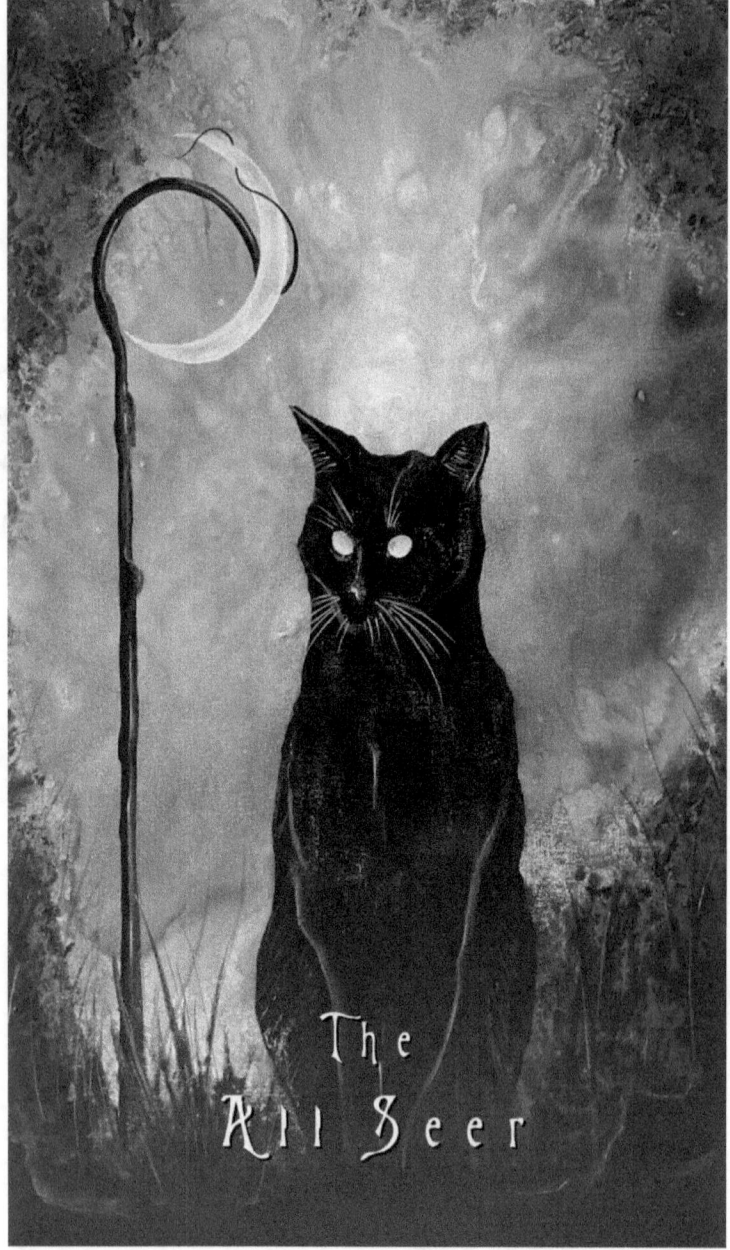

The All Seer

The All Seer

Keywords: Vision, Foresight, Realism

The All Seer is here.

It wants to show you something.

Actually...it wants to show you *everything*.

When this familiar shows up, it's a sign that you need to open your eyes wide to what's happening in your life. The All Seer reminds us that the truth is out there, and that all it takes is someone ready and willing to learn it.

If a person in your life has tried to deceive you or your loved ones, you need to see through the deception. If big changes in your life are coming, you must be prepared to anticipate the fallout. In doing so, you might learn a few difficult truths, but these are things you'll need to accept.

The All Seer is someone who can't be lied to, who doesn't accept half-answers or tricks, who isn't satisfied living a life of ignorance. Now is the time for the All Seer to become *you*.

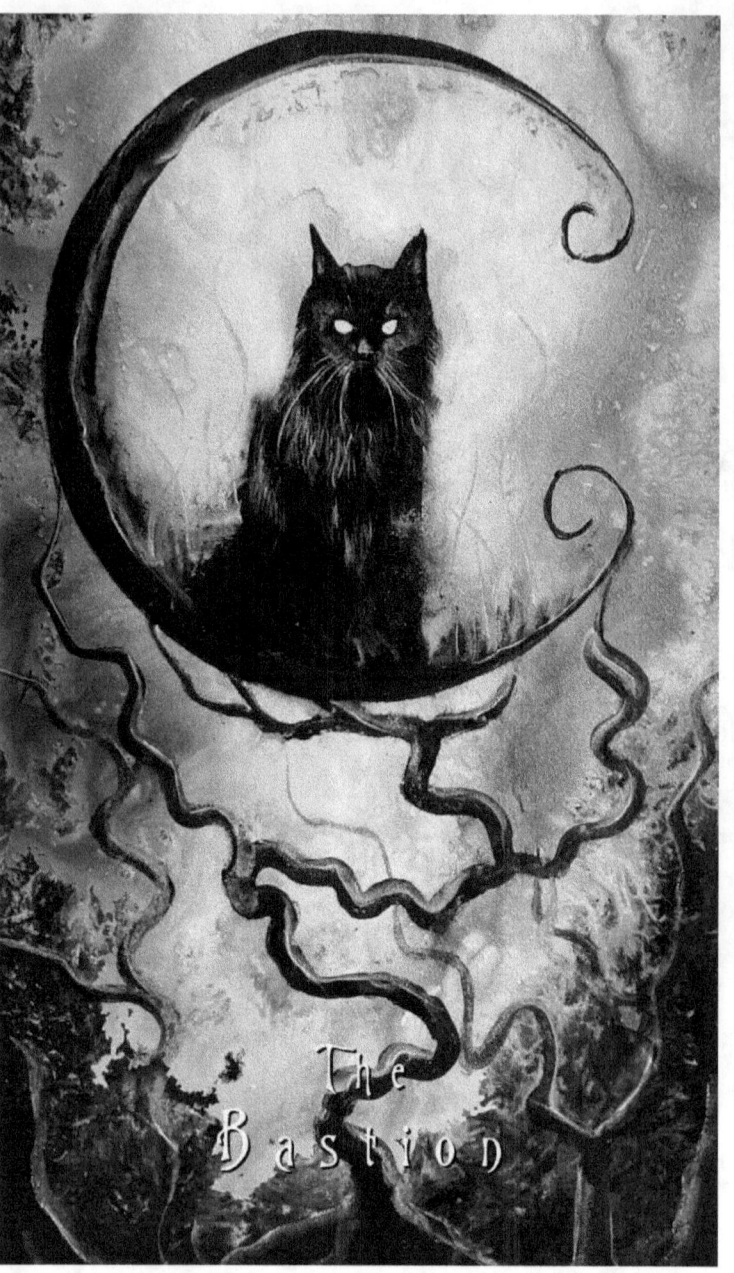

The
Bastion

The Bastion

Keywords: Defense, Walls, Resistance

If The Bastion comes to your card spread, you may find that you need to defend yourself.

There are times in life during which it's not appropriate to build high emotional walls. After all, being defensive all the time isn't generally healthy.

But today the time could be right to properly protect yourself. It may be that legal troubles loom, that someone is undermining you at work or home, or that some external threat has become too large to ignore. The Bastion wants you to not just defend yourself, but to do so vigorously. Put on your emotional armor, strap a truthful sword to your waist, and stand up for what's right.

As long as your cause is righteous, and as long as your heart is true, you cannot be defeated.

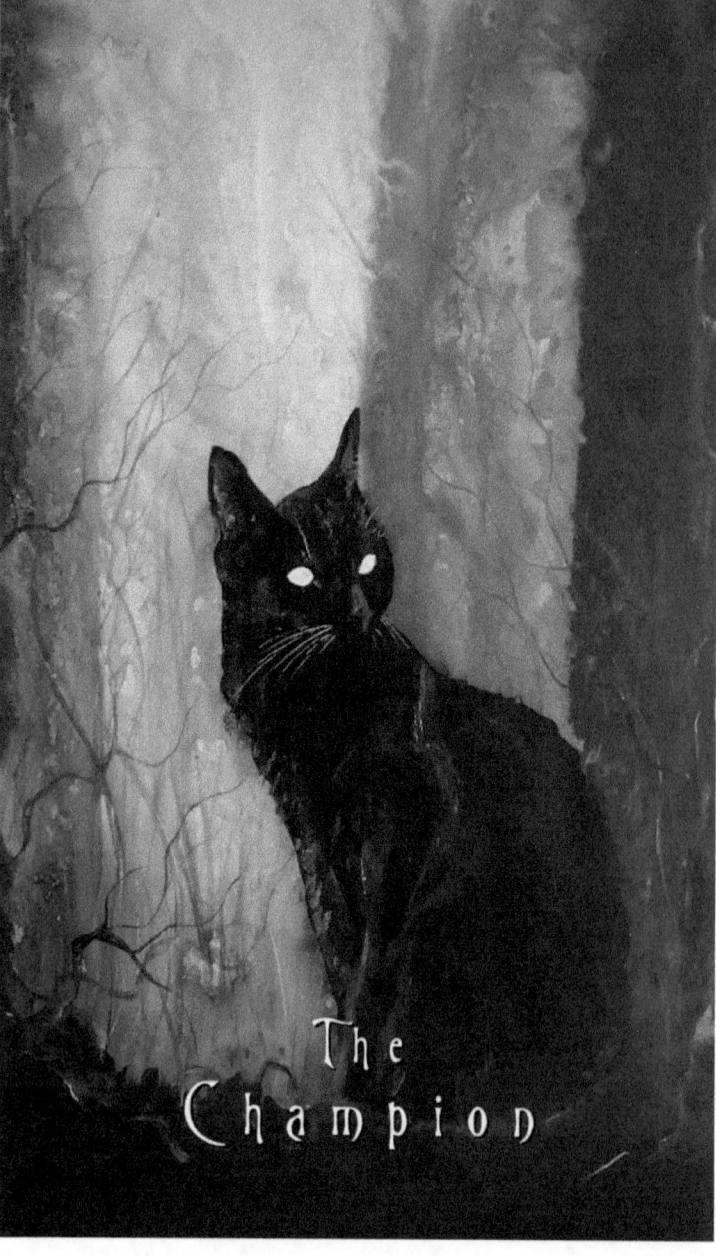

The
Champion

The Champion

Keywords: Bravery, Leadership, Honor

Sometimes we either need a champion in our lives.

Or...

We need to become one.

If you've pulled The Champion, it could be that you need someone to stick up for you, to lead the way, and to help you overcome a big obstacle. In other words, you need a hero.

Alternatively, you might need to take on these duties yourself, either for your own benefit or to help someone who is vulnerable. A family member, a friend, or even your partner could be in a state of weakness. And you might be the only one who can support them.

It's time to take a good, hard look at the state of things. Something needs overcoming. There's an obstacle in the way. The Champion reminds us not to rest on our laurels and hope it'll all work out by itself. Find a friend who can be your hero, or become the hero yourself.

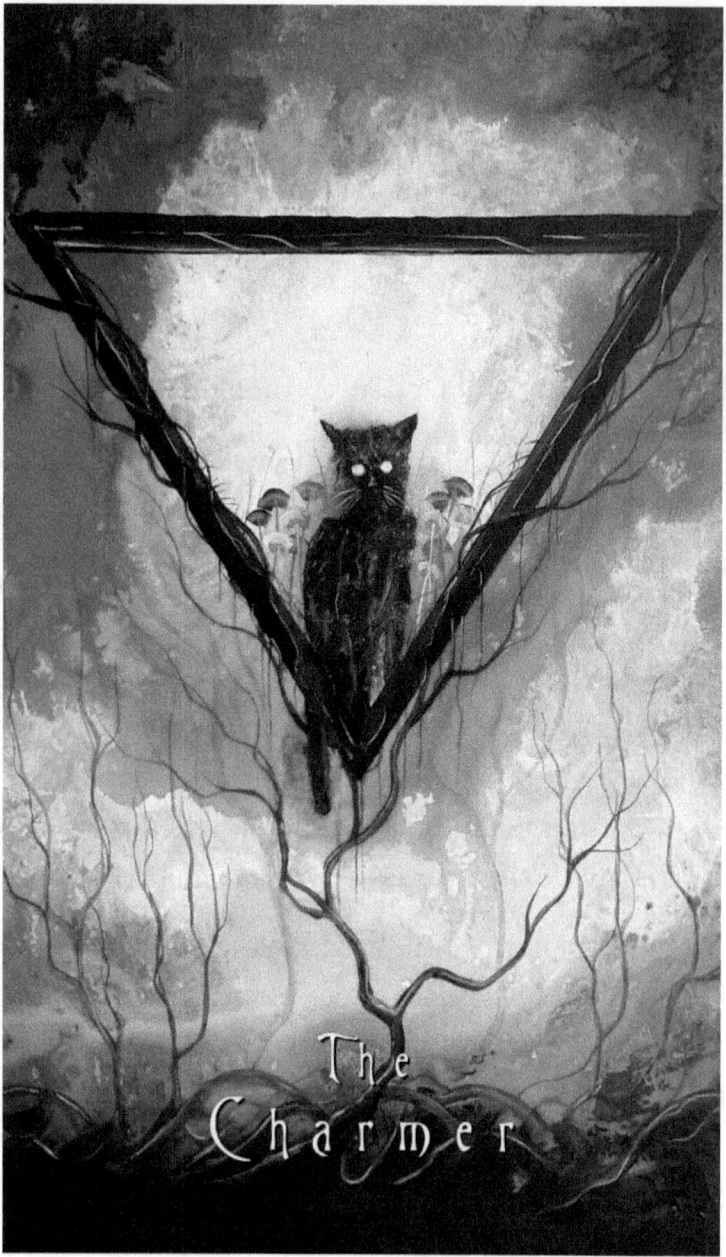

The
Charmer

The Charmer

Keywords: Allure, Attraction, Warmth

Need to win someone over?

Looking to make an impact at your place of work?

Just want to make someone smile?

The Charmer makes itself known when it's time for you to tap into your warm, fuzzy self. For some, wooing new friends and exerting influence on others comes naturally. But if this card shows up in your spread, it might be that you need a little reminder. Perhaps a situation in your life calls for more tact and diplomacy than usual. Or maybe you've grown a little hard around the edges of late.

The Charmer doesn't want you to manipulate people. Rather, it wants you to remember the good feelings of laughter and of true, soulful human connection. In many cases, positive things come from a softer, gentler approach. Be your charming self, and pleasantry will usually result.

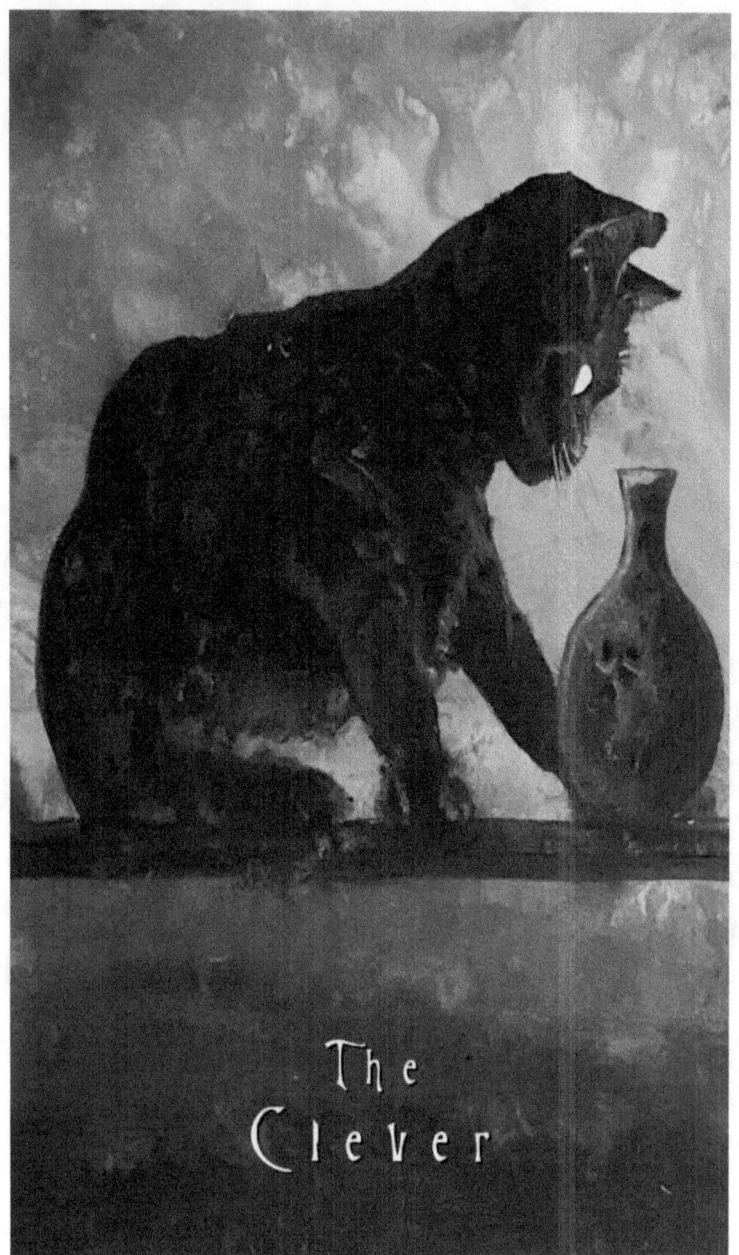

The
Clever

The Clever

Keywords: Intellect, Competence, Ideas

Sometimes it's best to use a scalpel, not a hammer.

What this means is—brute force isn't always the answer. Solutions to many problems require brains, not brawn.

The Clever arrives when it's time to use your wits. You might find yourself in a sticky life situation. A choice might need making. Money troubles or difficulty in your job or social life could be at hand.

Now is not the time to let emotions run the show. Tap into your inner genius, meditate on the challenge you're facing, and find the most rational solution.

The Clever reminds us that our greatest strength isn't in the power of our bodies, but instead in the adaptability of our minds.

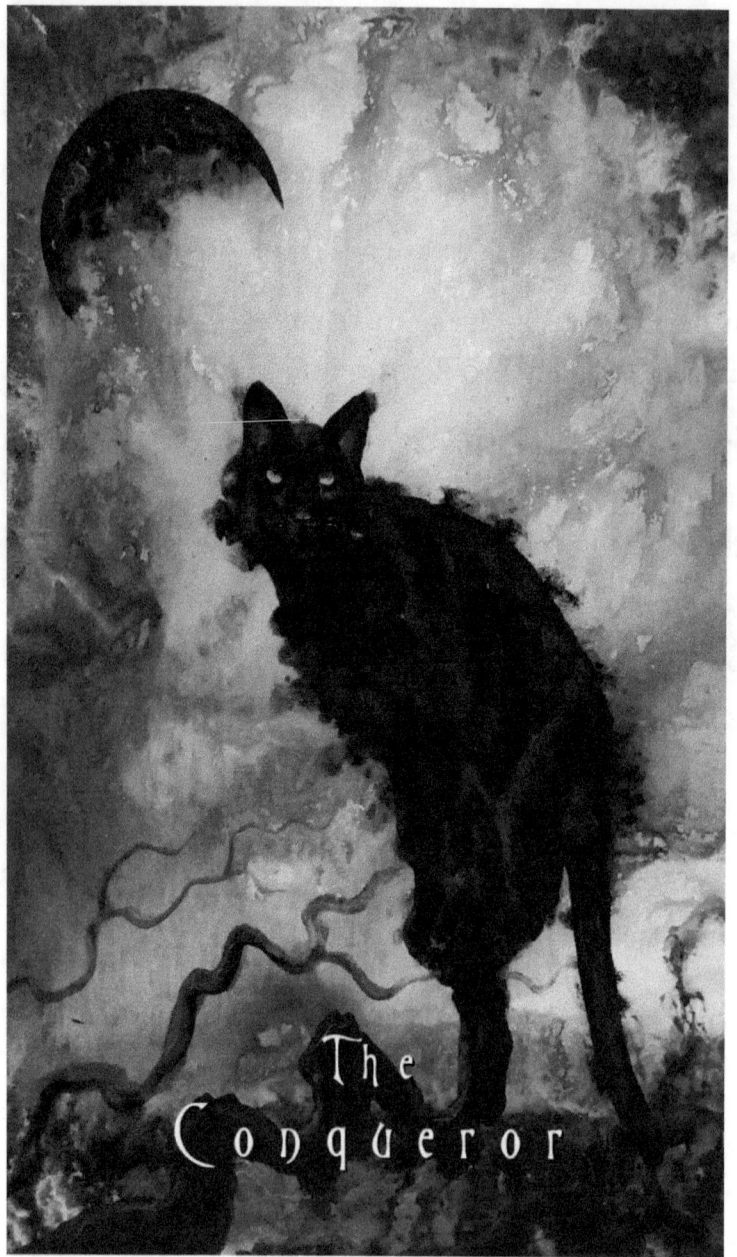

The
Conqueror

The Conqueror

Keywords: Confidence, Poise, Determination

The Conqueror reveals itself when the time is right for you to be your strongest self. Contrarily to The Clever or The Charmer, now could be the time for you to exert yourself forcefully.

If someone in your life needs confronting, it's time to face them head-on.

If a situation is getting out of hand, set aside all distractions and take control.

If you've set a goal, especially a big one, focus all of your energy on it until it's done.

The Conqueror reminds us that some things require a firm, steady hand. If it arrives in your card spread, consider the biggest challenges in your life...

...and conquer them.

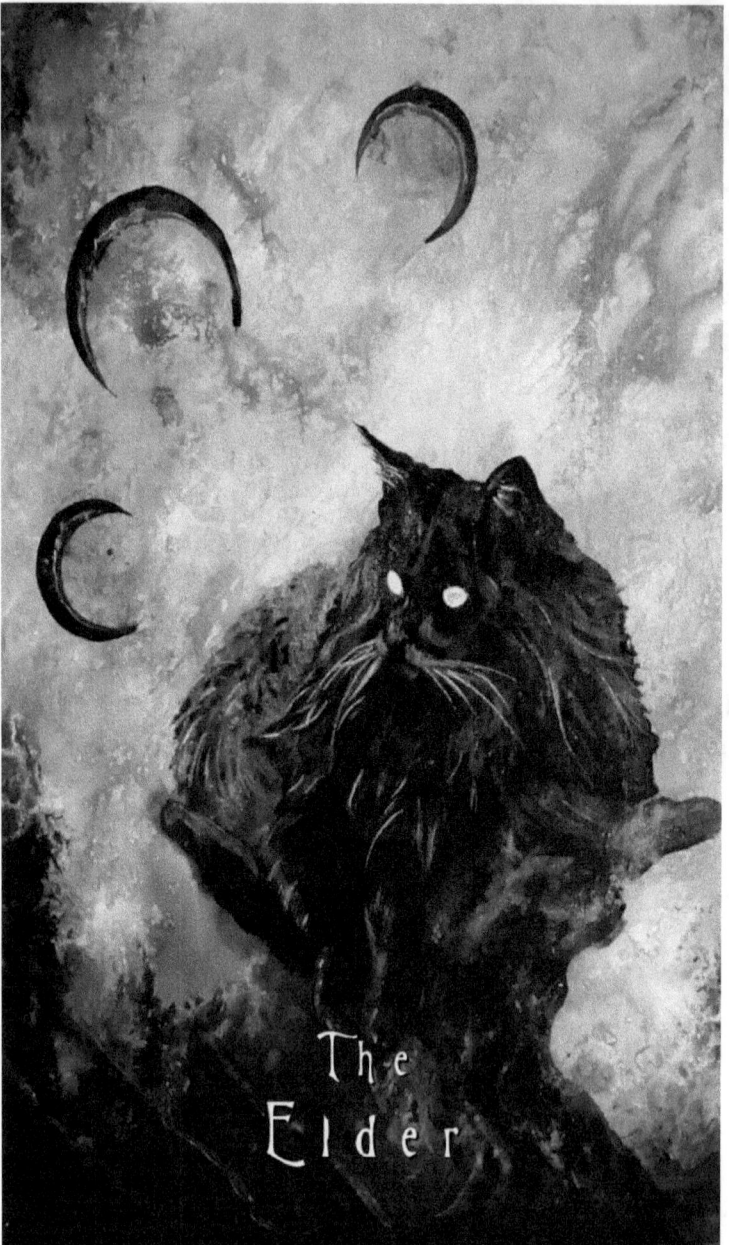

The
Elder

The Elder

Keywords: Wisdom, Guidance, Ancestry

Knowledge is simply knowing a thing. But wisdom is possessing the experience and perspective to put that knowledge to its best possible use.

If you've encountered The Elder, it's likely you're either in need of sage advice...or that you're in a position to help someone with an offering of your own wisdom.

In the former case, you may be seeking a mentor. You could find yourself in an unfamiliar setting, one in which an ounce of guidance would go a long way toward helping you. Don't be afraid to approach a parental figure, an elder in your family, or a friend with more experience than you.

In the latter situation, it could be you who is tasked with helping a novice, teaching a friend, or simply showing someone the ropes of a place unfamiliar to them. It's best to treat this responsibility with reverence. Your impact could change someone's life.

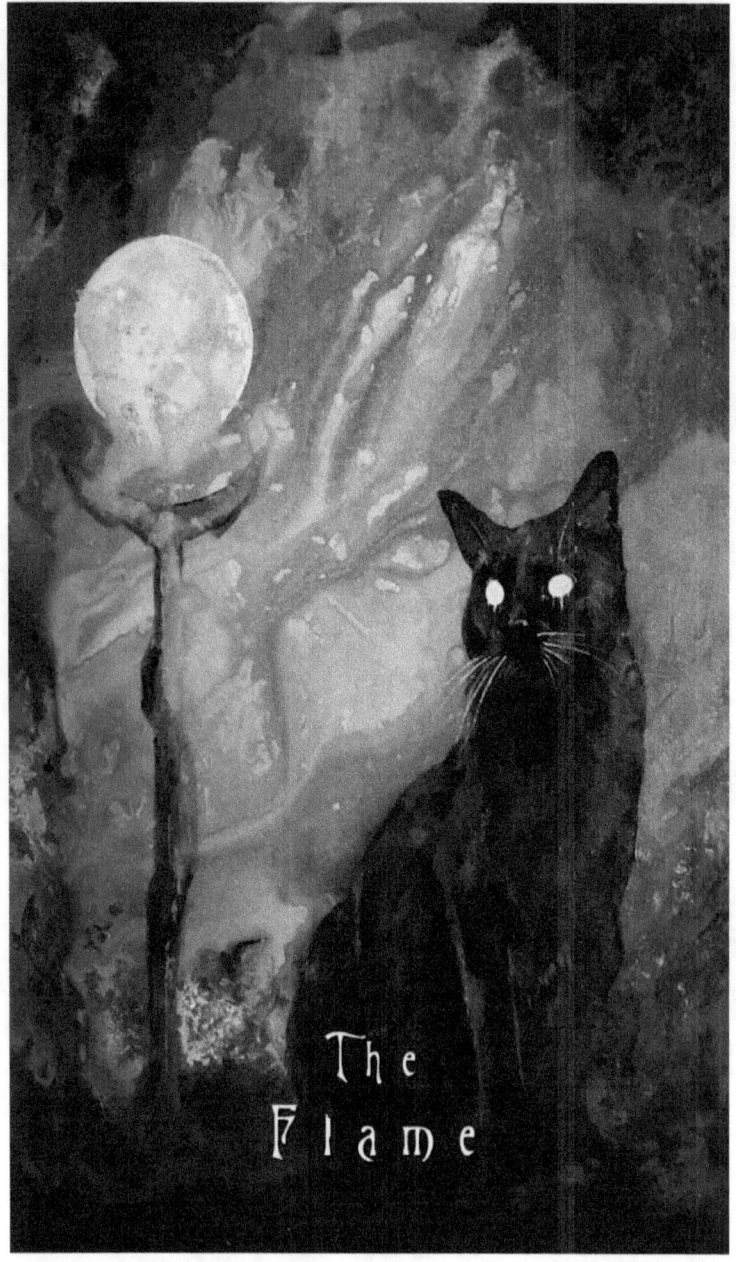

The Flame

Keywords: Motion, Freedom, Passion

Sometimes in life, it's best to release yourself of all constraint.

...to become as free as fire.

The Flame arrives when the moment is right for you to be your most passionate self. Whether in a new relationship, at your job, or in the throes of a big life change, now is the time to let your heart beat loudly and freely. Sitting still and taking caution is for another day. For the moment, desire has become your compass. Let it burn hot and unquenchable.

The Flame reminds us that not all moments in life are best approached calmly. There are times when your inner bonfire will need feeding. While making sure not to burn anyone else, it's important to let yourself feel free, independent of limits.

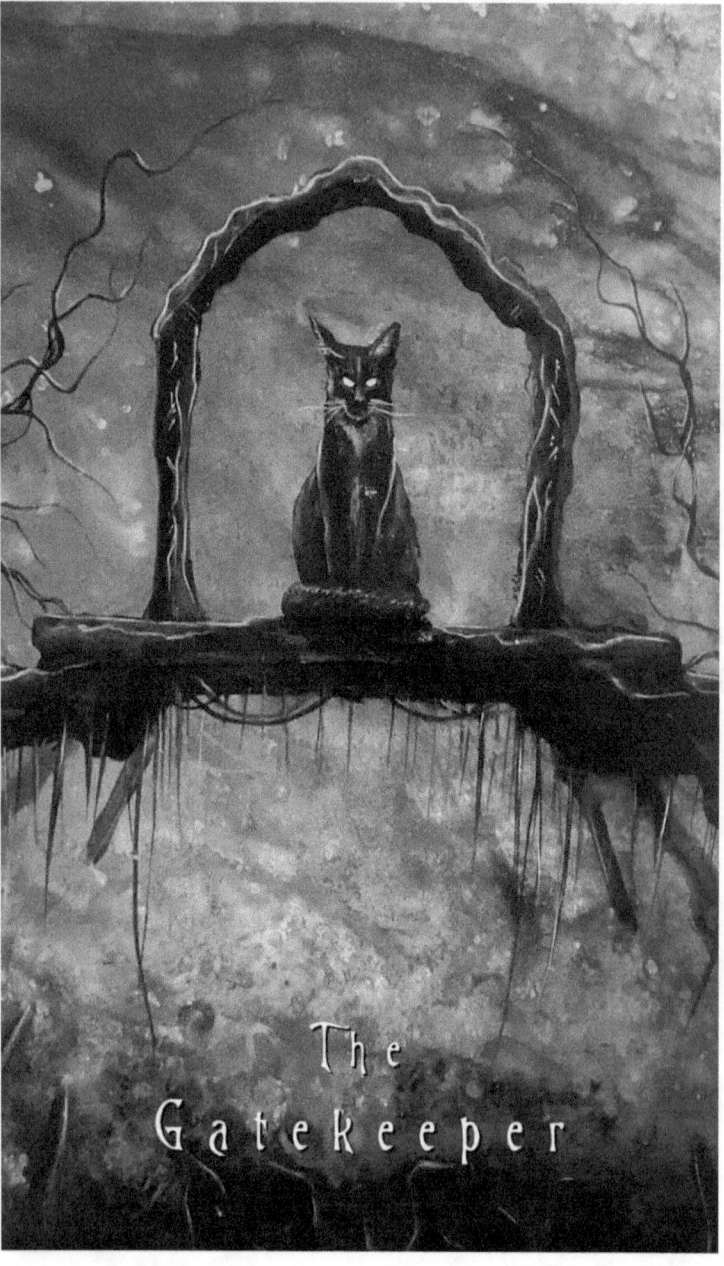

The
Gatekeeper

The Gatekeeper

Keywords: Vigilance, Discerning, Attentive

If The Gatekeeper makes its presence known, it's probable you're going through a time in your life during which you're being choosy, even picky.

Whether for better or worse, you're not in the mood to let everyone and everything into your life. The Gatekeeper stands vigilant watch at the door to your soul, rejecting anything which doesn't deserve to be invited inside.

This could be because your heart has been wounded recently.

Or because you're feeling distrustful of a new person in your orbit.

Or it could be that your intuition is particularly sharp right now, and it's time to be extra-attentive.

The Gatekeeper wants to keep out any and all negative influences in your life. Just remember not to block out the good along with the bad.

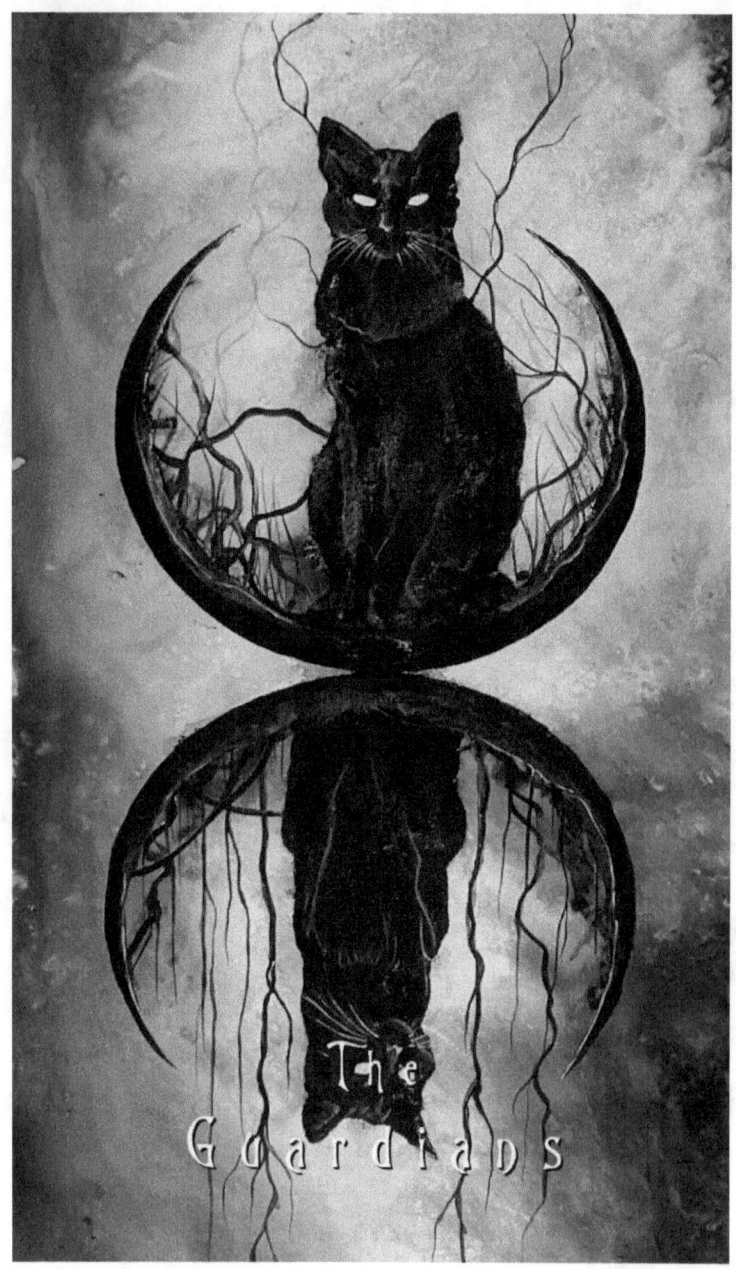

The Guardians

Keywords: Protection, Shielding, Avoidance

The twin familiars of The Guardians make themselves known when you are in some sort of danger. They're meant to guard both your body and your mind, and to allow no physical or emotional harm to come to you.

If this card has come to you, it may be that you are engaging in risky behavior. You could be in peril of physical danger, of at risk of being taken advantage of by another person...or *both*. The Guardians desire to protect you, not necessarily by removing you from all risk, but by increasing your awareness of it.

It is, of course, impossible to move through the world without assuming any risk. That said, The Guardians intend to open your eyes about the true nature of the hazards before you. Whether you're skydiving, driving without your seatbelt, or *dating*, they want your eyes open and your head clear. In most cases, simple awareness of danger is enough to minimize it.

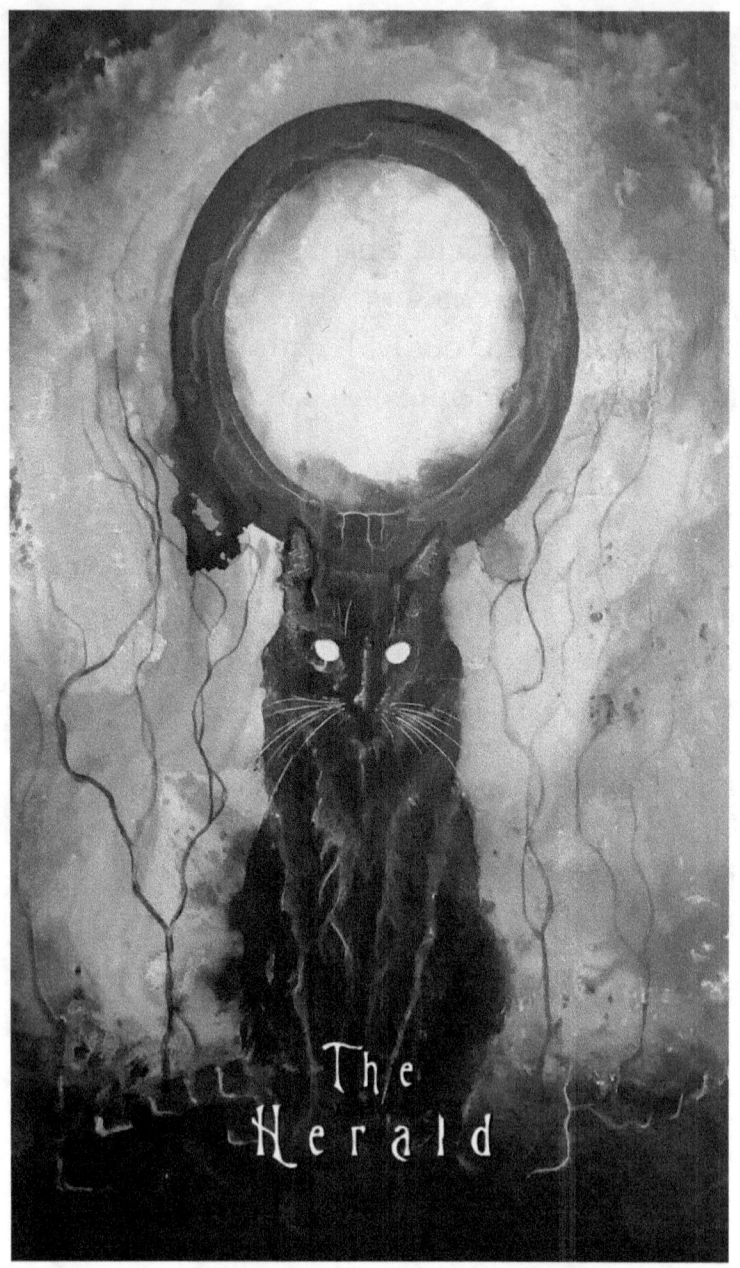

The Herald

The Herald

Keywords: Messenger, Augury, Omen

When The Herald appears, it's a clear sign that someone or something is trying to get your attention. If you feel a nagging sensation that something big is about to happen, you might want to pay closer attention to your surroundings. If someone's been giving you advice or trying (but failing) to spend time with you, it could be time to listen to them, and to open your schedule for them.

The key here is *availability*. For a change, don't ignore your incoming phone calls. If a friend wants face-time, give it to them. The universe itself might be trying to deliver a message to you, and you'd be wisest not to ignore it.

While the meaning of the message could be just about anything, what's important is to let it through. Don't shoot the messenger. All The Herald asks is that you clear your mind and listen closely.

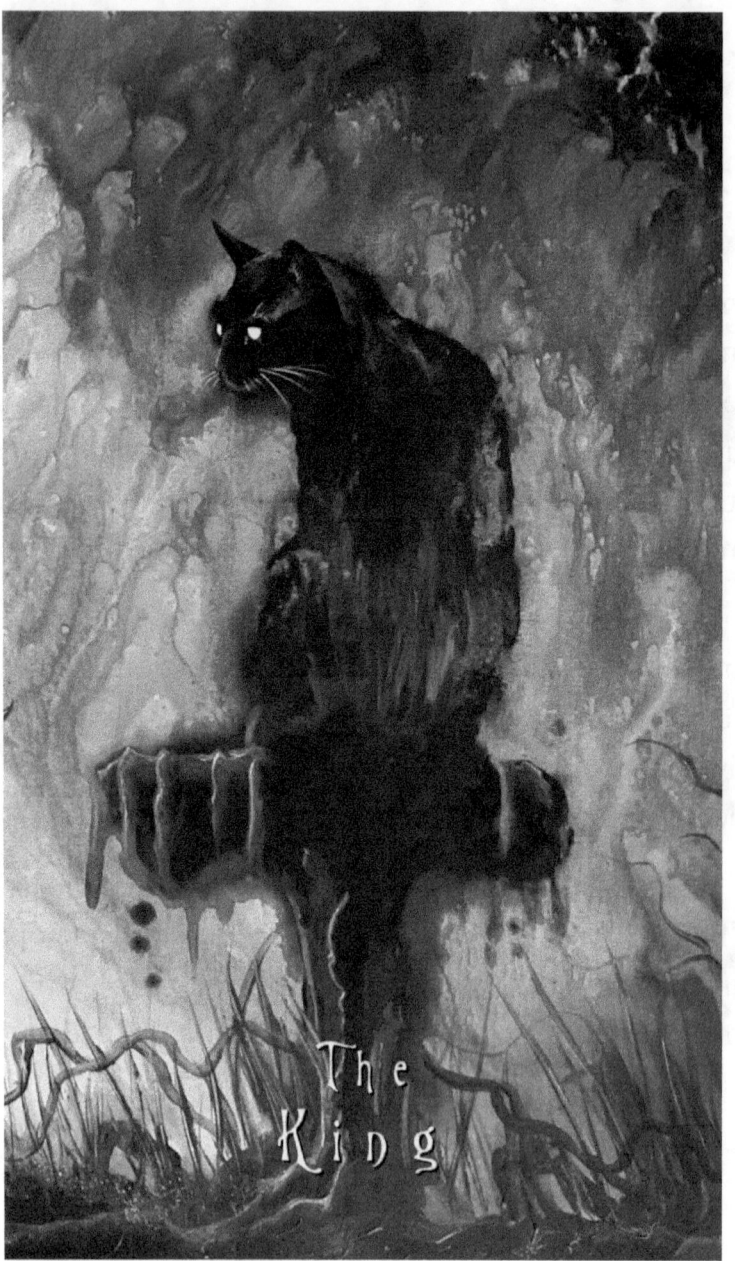

The King

Keywords: Masculine, Fatherly, Provider

The King is the embodiment of masculine energy. If he's appeared, it's time for you to get in touch either with your own masculine side or to seek out a patriarchal figure among your friends and family for guidance.

It could be that it's time for you to seize the reins and provide financially for those around you.

Or to take a new student under your wing, teaching them the virtues of honor, courage, and discipline.

Or perhaps your focus needs to be more personal. Money, leadership, assertiveness...these could be areas in which your attention is needed.

Or it could be a male figure in your life has something important to show you.

The King wants to guide you on a path of inner strength. Harness your experience, your determination, and your willingness to be better in all you do.

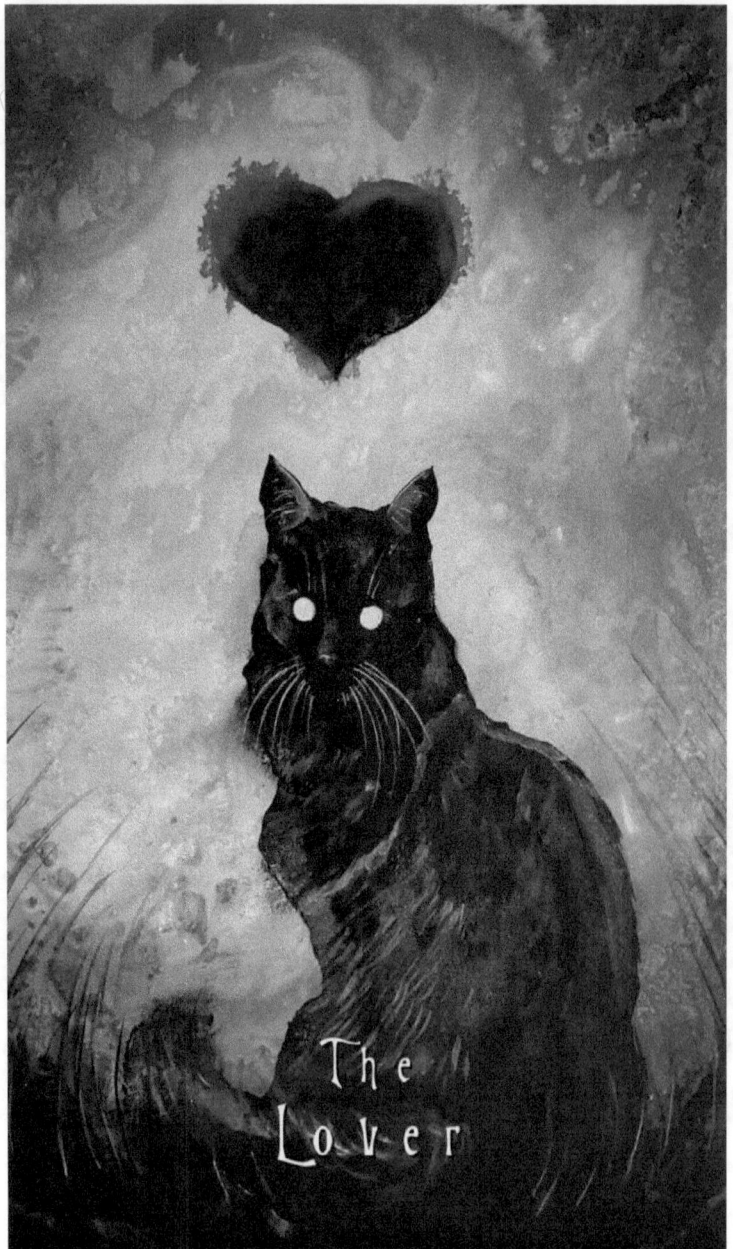

The Lover

Keywords: Romance, Desire, Temptation

The Lover is what you suspect. If this familiar slips into your card spread, something could be brewing in your heart.

It may be that you have a choice to make regarding a romantic relationship. One lover, or even several, could be knocking at your door, and now you must decide what to do about it.

The Lover could also portend a new (and often exciting) romantic entanglement is near. You may find yourself tempted by someone you didn't expect.

Lastly, The Lover could signal the end of a relationship. In this case, The Lover is acting as a protector, shielding your heart from the pain of wounds suffered due to a romance turned sour.

The Lover reminds us to balance our wants against our needs, and to weigh the nurturing of our hearts against the desire of our bodies.

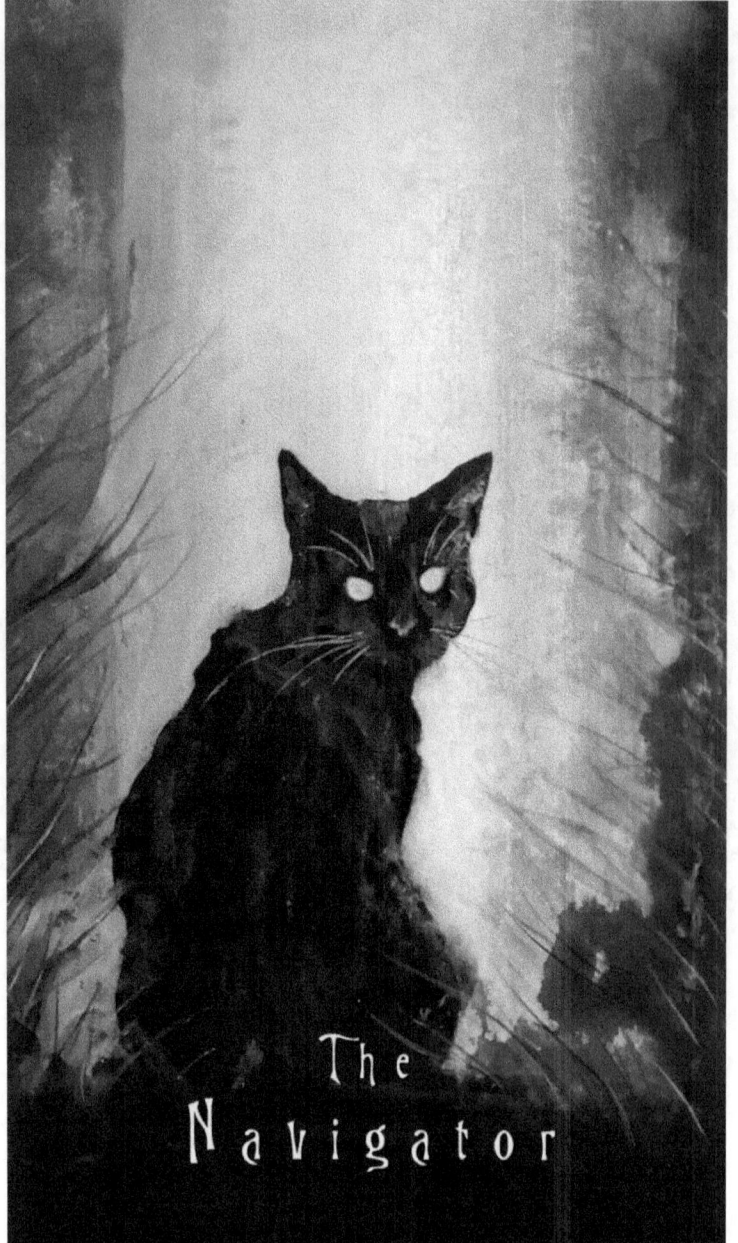

The Navigator

The Navigator

Keywords: Guidance, Instructions, Counseling

The Navigator is the same as a ship's captain on stormy seas. Though the waves may be high, the winds powerful, and the shores far away, this familiar will see you to safety...if you allow it.

When The Navigator sails into your sights, it's time to remain steady. If you're in the midst of a big project, don't despair. Seek the aid of others if you can, and don't be afraid to follow the path of those who came before you. At this time in your life, there's no need to reinvent the wheel. You'll reach your goals faster not by resisting the winds of change, but by accepting that many have taken this journey before you.

The time to forge your own path and exert your highest level of creativity will come...but not today. Now is the time to stay the course and to follow the river where it takes you.

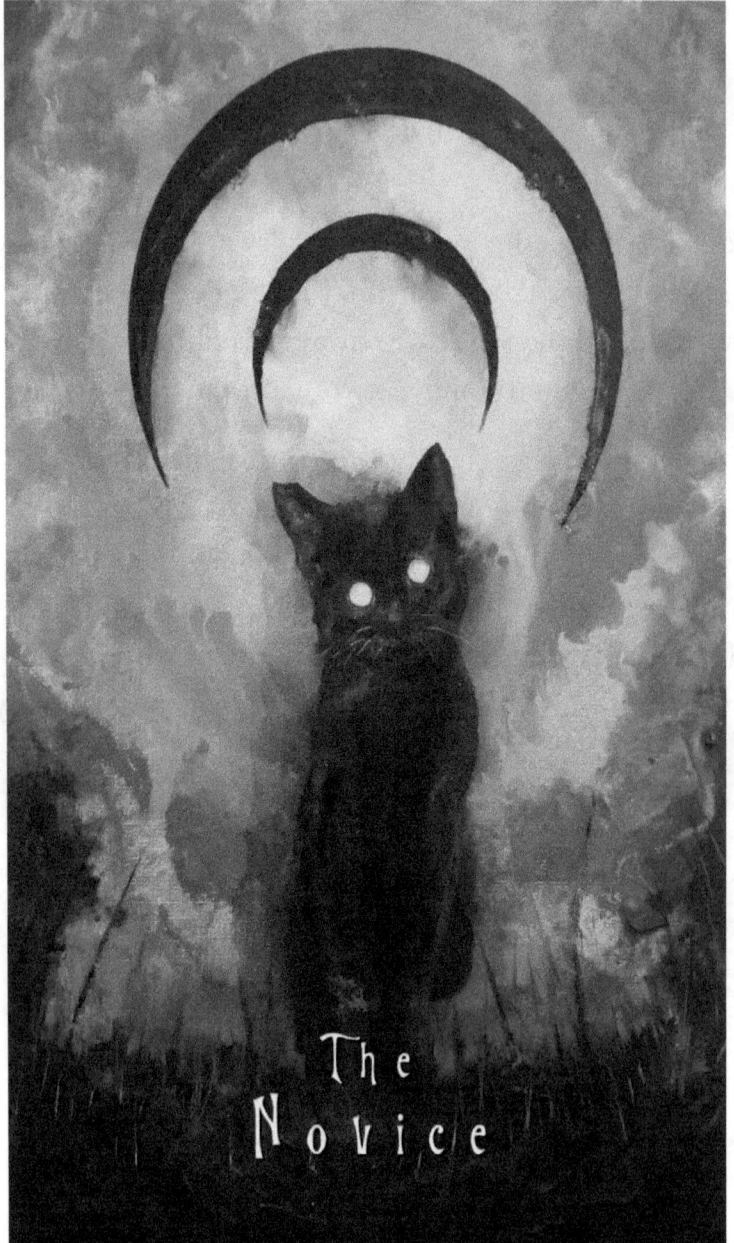

The Novice

The Novice

Keywords: Youth, Newbie, Enthusiasm

Are you ready for adventure?

The Novice hopes so.

This familiar appears when something so new and fresh is upon you, you might not know what to do.

Perhaps you've moved to a new location, accepted a new job, or started learning a skill you've never before tried. Whatever the case, a sense of newness is either already upon you or just around the corner.

You might be anxious about it. Or outright afraid. The Novice is here to walk beside you and remind you that although you've taken a big leap into something new, you're going to be fine. Once you overcome the first hurdles, your fears could become passions, and your worries will melt away.

The Novice reminds us to try new things as often as possible, and to go boldly into new situations.

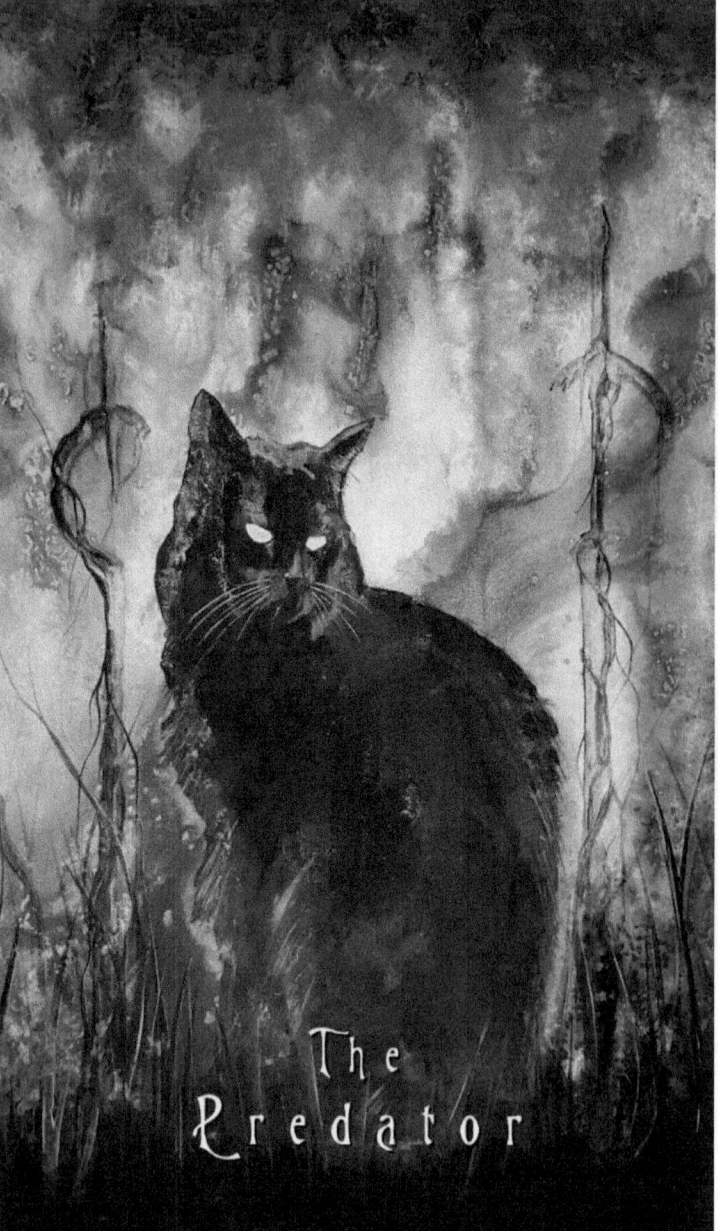

The
Predator

The Predator

Keywords: Initiative, Aggression, Directness

The Predator is unlike most of the other familiars.

It doesn't want to protect you, at least not in the usual ways.

If you've pulled The Predator, it's a hint that the time for sitting back and allowing things to happen is over. If you're patiently waiting for something good to come, if you're daydreaming, if you're always hoping, but rarely doing, this is your time to change.

Be the aggressor. That's not meant in a violent sense, of course. Rather, The Predator wants you to take the initiative, to strike first, and to become (for at least this one moment) the pack leader.

This card reminds us that sometimes, when something has to be done just right, you need to do it yourself, and you need to do it *now.*

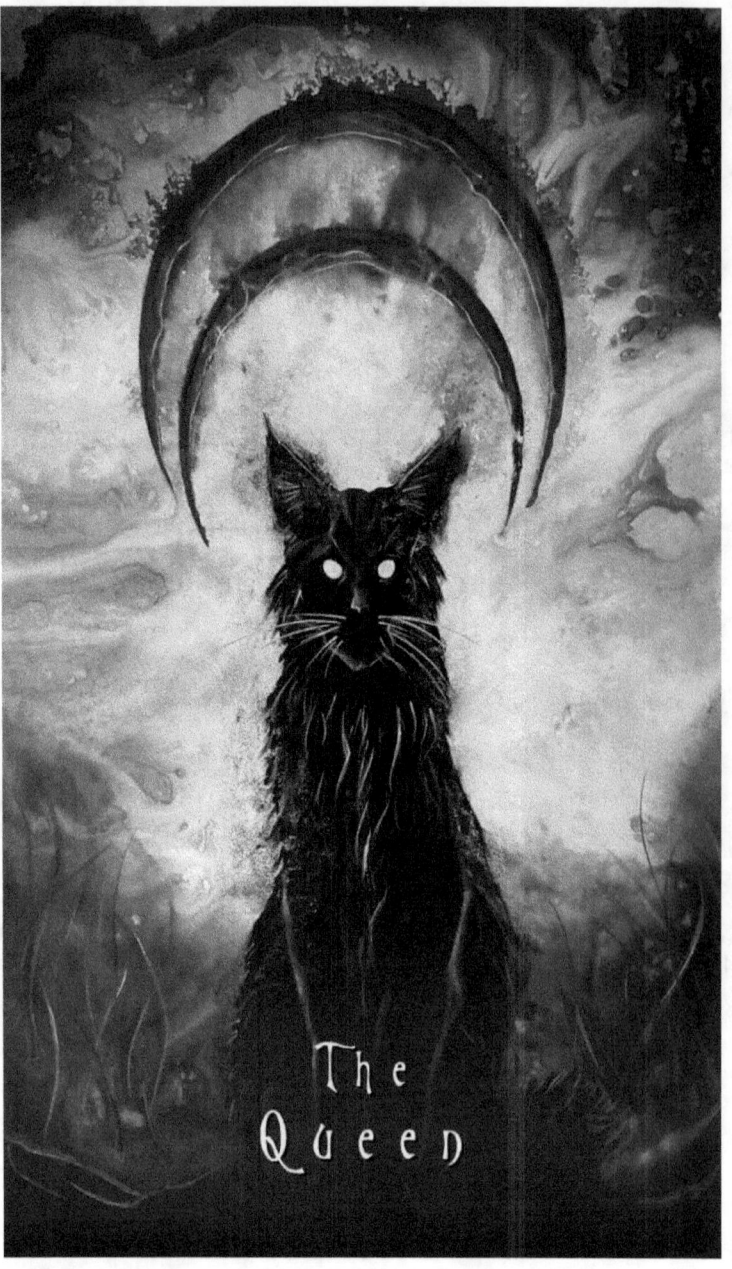

The
Queen

The Queen

Keywords: Feminine, Nurturing, Protective

The Queen is the embodiment of feminine energy. If she's appeared, it's time to tap into your caring, emotional side or to seek out a matriarchal figure in your life for guidance.

It could be that it's time for you to help or care for a younger person or a close friend.

Or to mentor someone in need, teaching them the virtues of wisdom, spirituality, and wisdom.

Or perhaps your focus should be more personal. Intuition, protection, overcoming emotional turmoil...these could be areas in which your attention is needed.

Or it could be a female figure in your life has something important to show you.

The Queen wants to guide you on a path of inner strength and spirituality. Harness your experience, your wisdom, and your love.

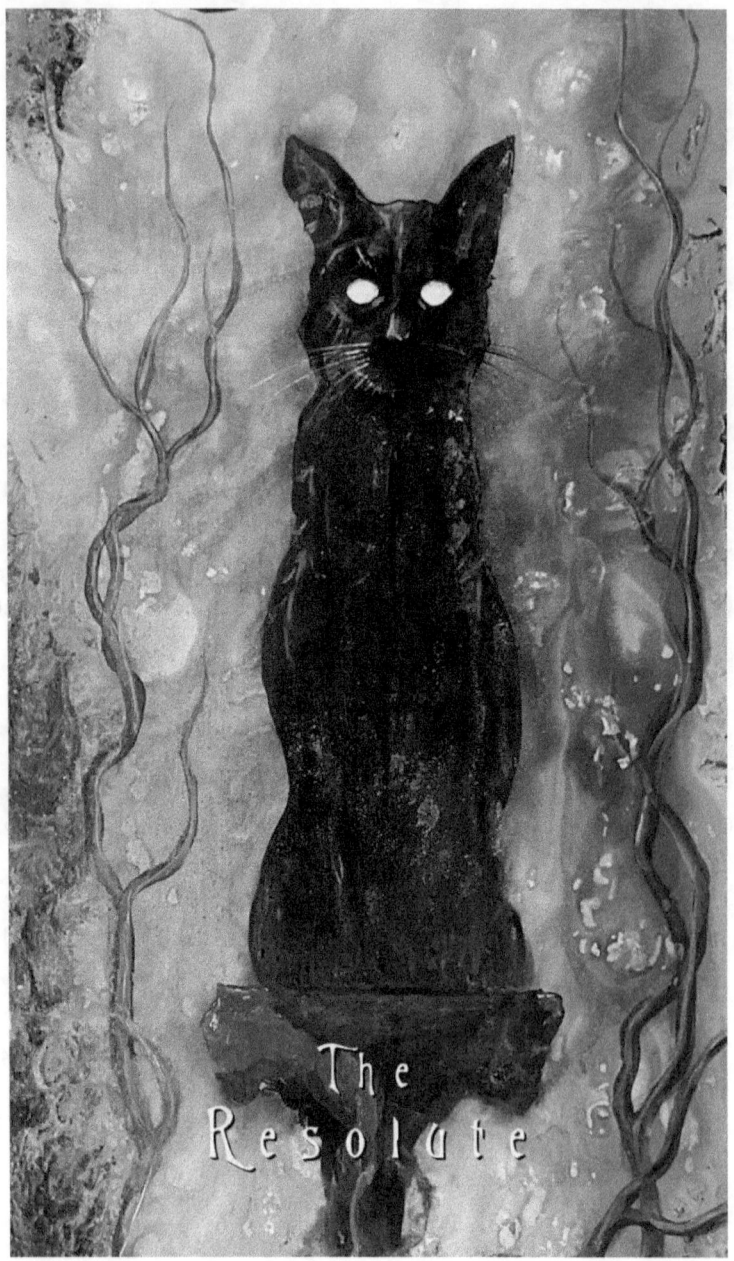

The
Resolute

The Resolute

Keywords: Acceptance, Diligence, Single-Mindedness

The final stage is acceptance...or so goes the saying.

If this familiar shows its face, it could mean one of two things.

1. You've decided to strive toward a new goal, something which will require your focus for a long time to come.
2. You recently (or you're about to) reach the final stage of grief or some other emotional turmoil, which means you will soon be required to accept a difficult truth.

In either case, The Resolute wants to be your guide. If you've decided to pursue a new and challenging goal, this familiar wants to push you, support you, and remind you of your own inner strength. The more difficult the goal, the stronger your determination must be.

If a difficult truth requiring acceptance is near, The Resolute wants you to reach it with a sense of purpose. Do not fear the truth. Embrace it.

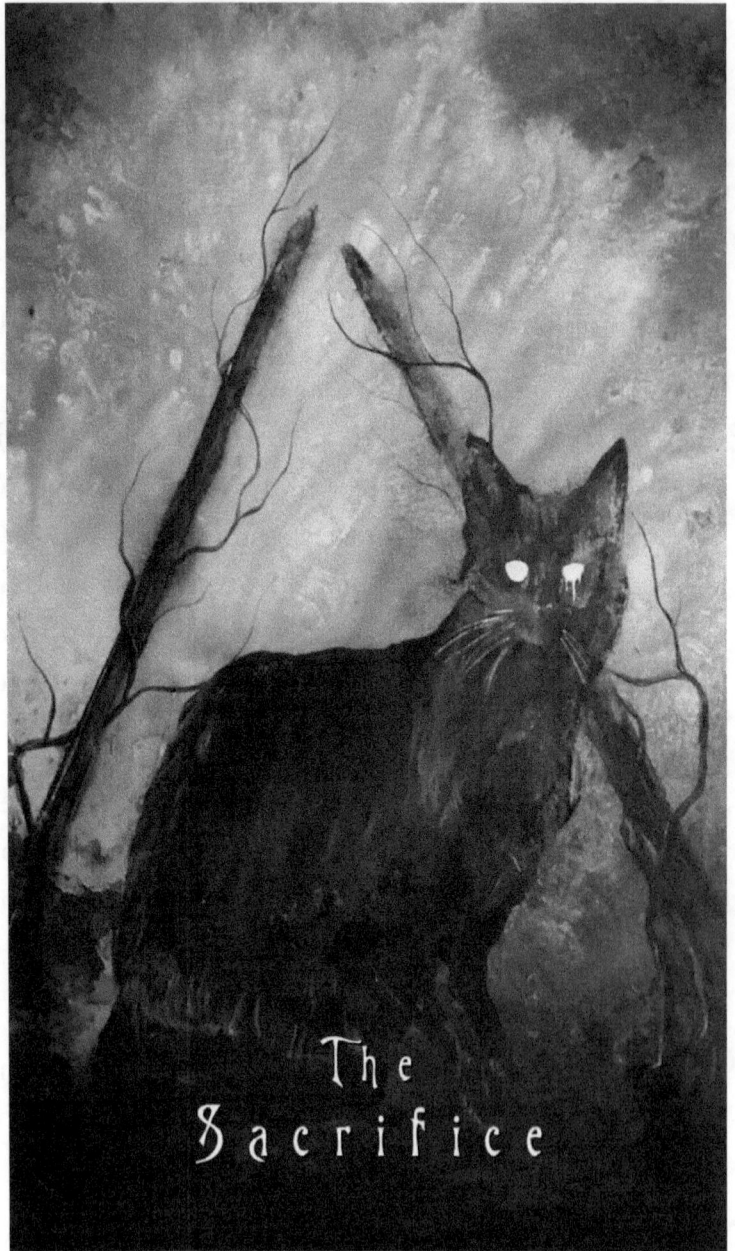

The
Sacrifice

The Sacrifice

Keywords: Giving, Unselfish, Humility

One of life's greatest challenges is to give without the expectation of receiving something in return.

If The Sacrifice is revealed to you, an opportunity to give of yourself could be at hand. Someone in your life may be in dire need. You may be even called upon to put away your pride and ego, and to listen, not speak.

However this opportunity arrives in your life, The Sacrifice wants to remind you that giving of yourself is one of life's highest honors. Making offerings that can never be repaid are rewarding in that they enrich your soul.

This familiar doesn't want you to make a martyr of yourself or to suffer senselessly. Rather, it desires that you choose the right moment to be generous and to set aside self-concern for the benefit of others.

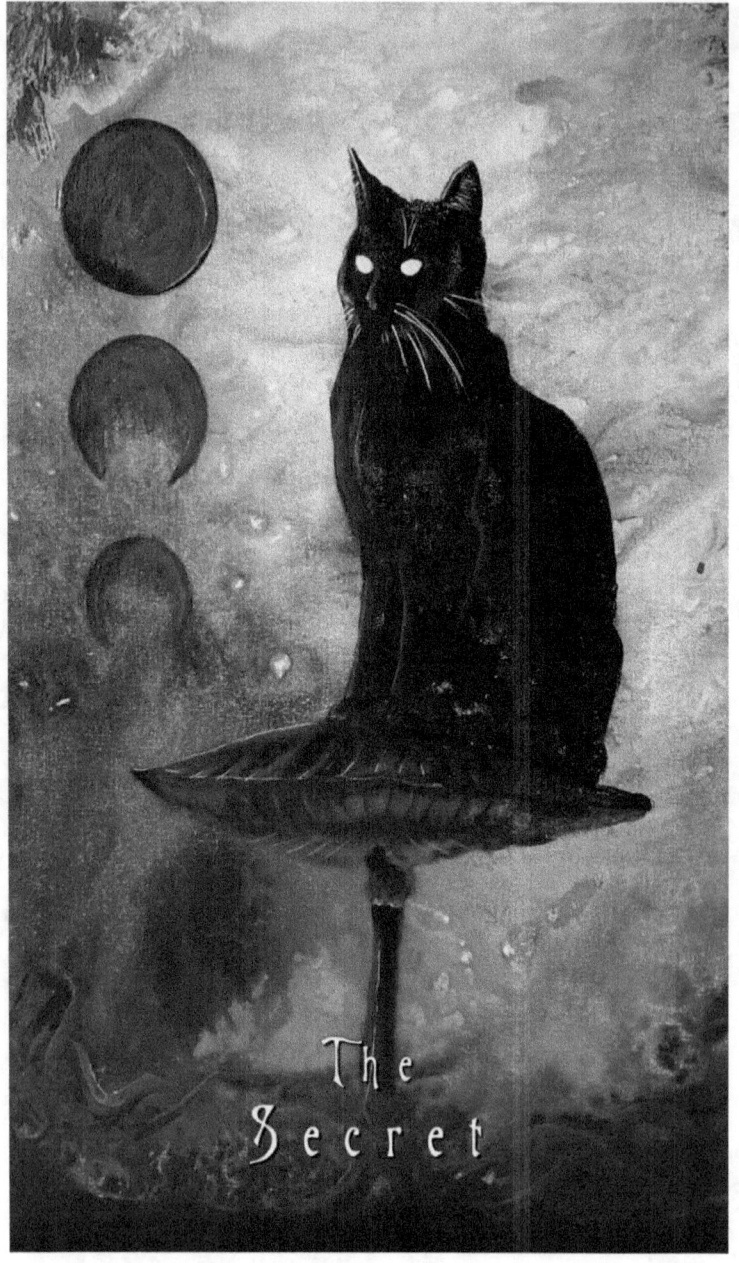

The
Secret

The Secret

Keywords: Privacy, Honesty, Confidential

When The Secret arrives in your card spread, it's for your own good.

A friend or family member may be trusting you with a private matter of utmost importance. Or an exciting piece of information might have landed on your doorstep.

In any event, now is not the time to open up or breach anyone's trust. Keep things close to your chest, no matter how tempted you might be to reveal what you know. Sometimes, less is more. When it comes to self-preservation, it's often better to remain silent until the perfect moment presents itself.

The Secret reminds us not to overshare and to always honor sacred truths told to us in confidence.

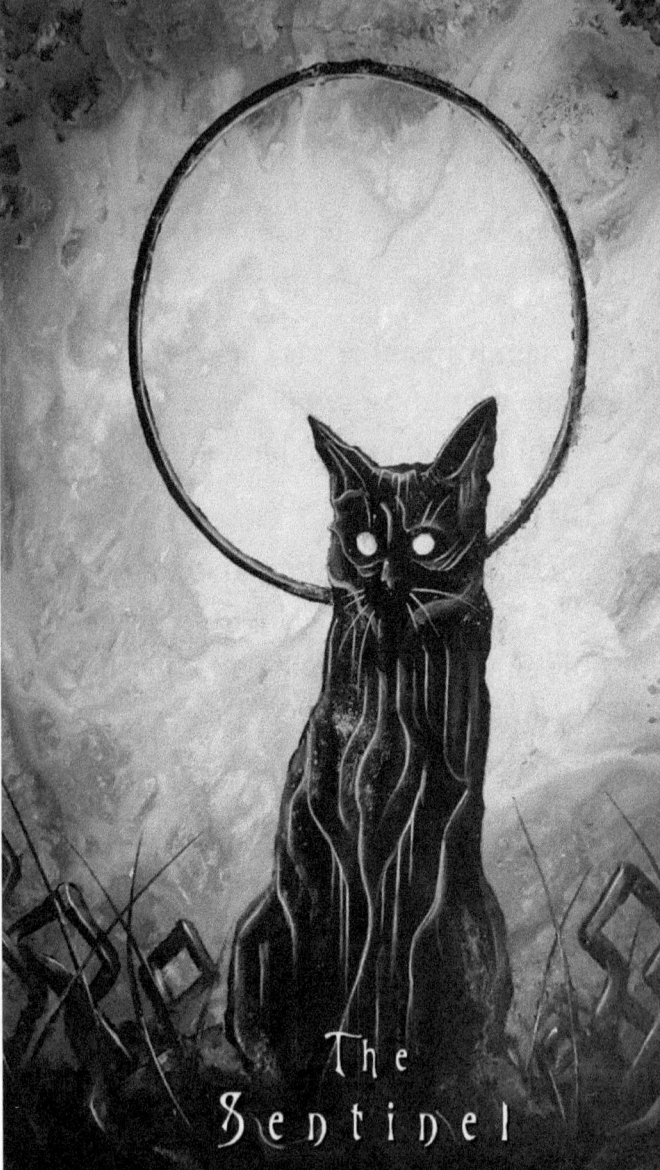

The
Sentinel

The Sentinel

Keywords: Observant, Guarded, Control

Everyone needs someone to watch their back.

The Sentinel reveals itself when yours is in need of watching.

When this familiar arrives, it likely signals that something is changing (or will soon change) in your life. A marriage, a divorce, a big move, or a shakeup in your financial situation. During this period of transition, you may be tempted to let the cards fall as they may, to leave things at least partly to chance.

But the Sentinel wants you to keep a closer eye.

Now is the time to cross your T's and dot your I's. Dig deep, remain vigilant, and steer your upcoming life change in a direction that feels right. When everything settles, you'll want to be in a better place than you previously were.

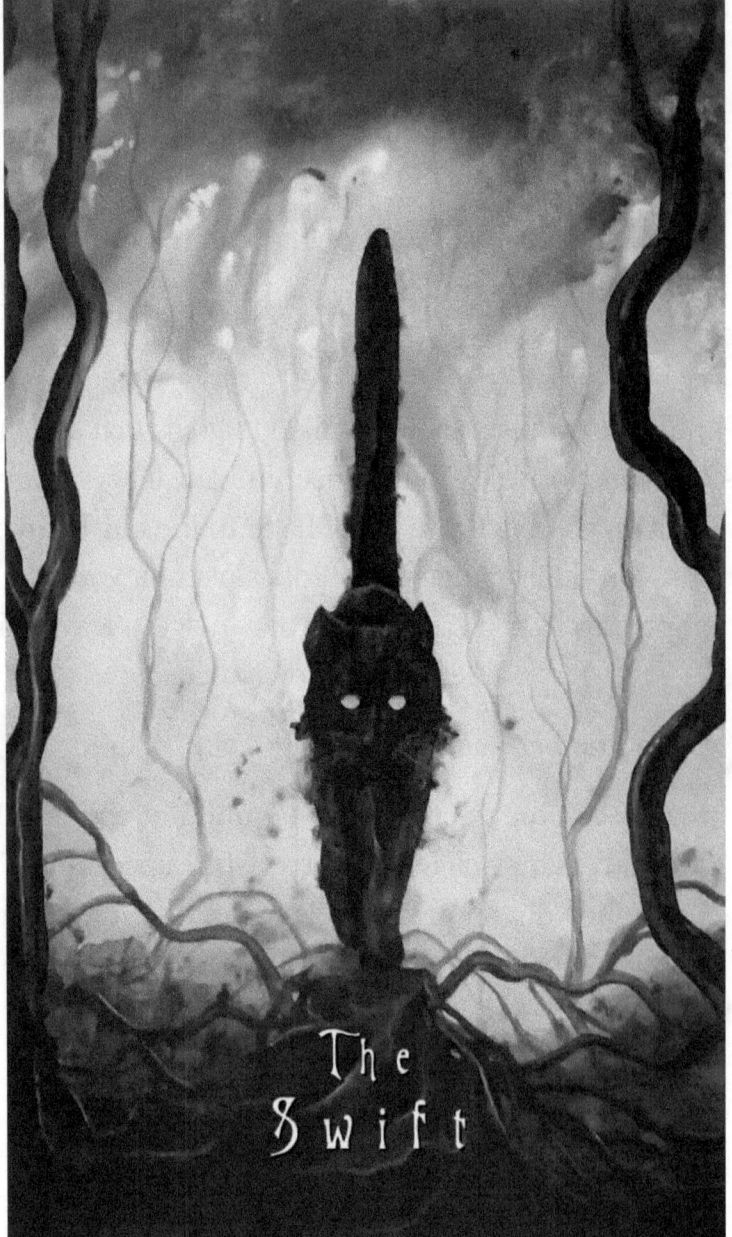

The
Swift

The Swift

Keywords: Quickness, Flexibility, Cutting-Edge

The early bird gets the worm...or so someone once said.

The Swift has a simple, direct message for you. *Be first.* If you're working a challenging job, be first to the jobsite. If you've got a romantic date coming up, arrive early. If you've got a difficult task to be done, finish it now and relax later.

When this familiar arrives in your card spread, it's time for maximum effort. Some goals in life can be met with mere coasting or by sticking to a comfortable routine. But when The Swift shows up, it's time to accelerate to the next level. Striving for absolute perfection isn't what's needed at the moment. Staying in motion and letting others see your raw effort is the key.

The Swift reminds us to steer clear of procrastination, and that the most important steps in life are often the very first ones we take.

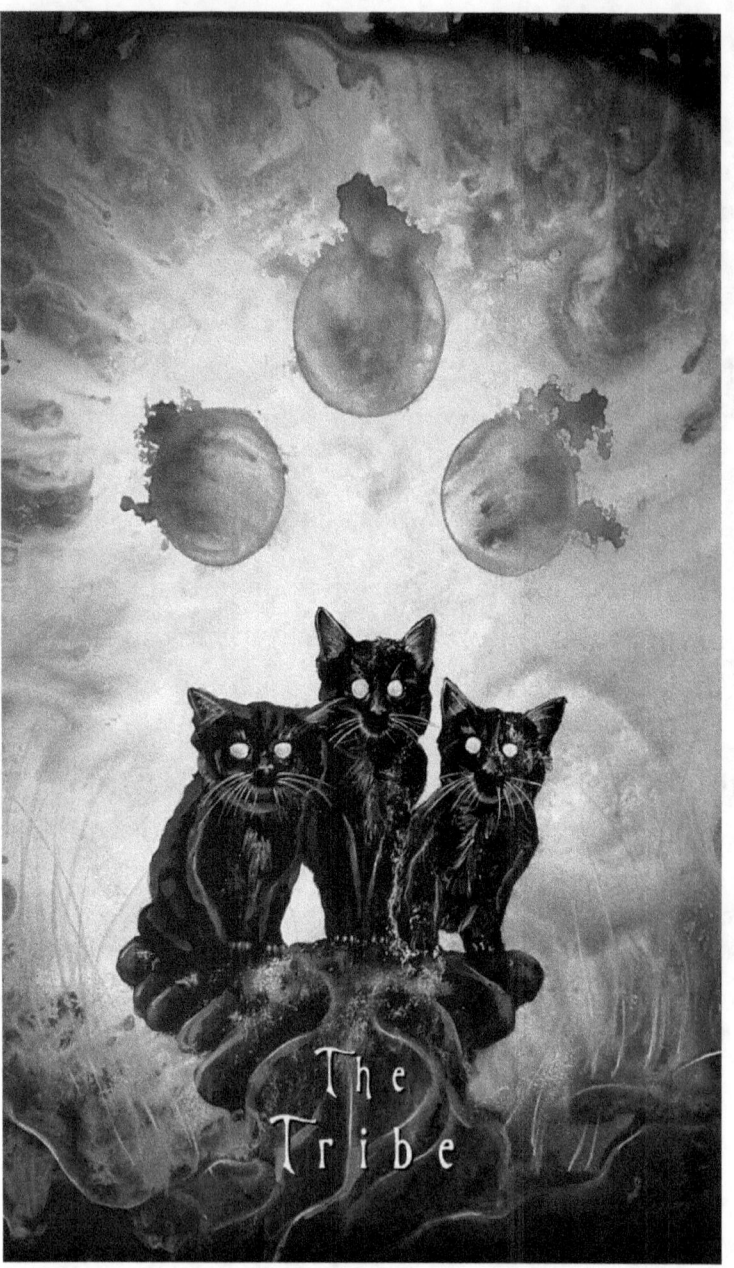

The
Tribe

The Tribe

Keywords: Friendship, Companions, Strength in Numbers

If and when you pull The Tribe, it's time to remember the old adage:

It takes a village.

It may be that you've been going at it alone for a while. Your sense of independence might be strong at the moment, if not particularly rewarding. If you encounter The Tribe in your reading, it's likely time for a change.

Spend more time with family and friends.

Invite others to participate in your latest project.

Gather up your team and head out into the world as a unified force.

The Tribe reminds that while success may come to us when we work alone, strength in numbers is a very real phenomenon. Now is the time for friendship, collaboration, and unity.

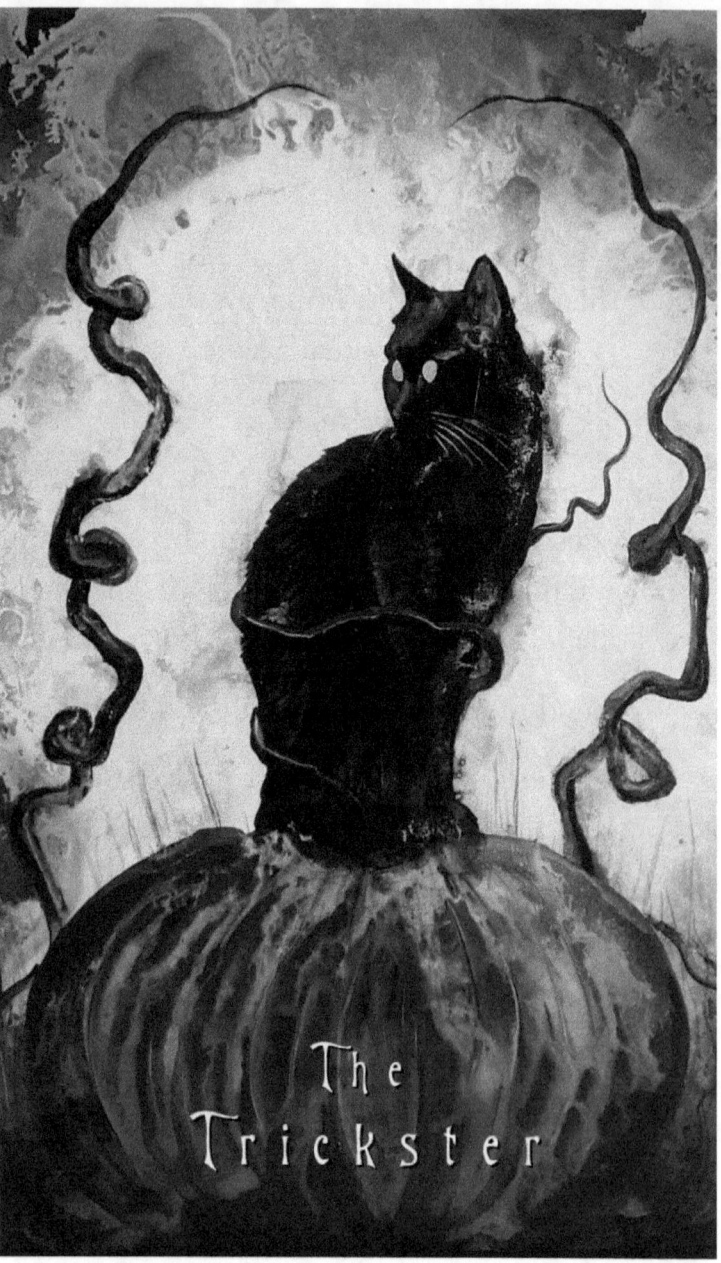

The
Trickster

The Trickster

Keywords: Cunning, Nimble, Indirect

The Trickster isn't here to deceive *you*, of course.

Nor does she wish you to trick or manipulate others.

When this familiar slides into your card spread, the moment may be right for you to be creative, crafty, and to take the long way around, rather than move in the most direct path. It's time to avoid trouble, not confront it headlong.

It may be that a certain situation in your life right now requires maximum tact, diplomacy, and possibly even the withholding of information. You may find yourself in a vulnerable or compromising state, not necessarily of your own making. The Trickster wants you to tap into your wily, witty self to escape trouble.

Alternatively, when this familiar appears, it may be that someone else is playing the role of trickster in your life. In such a case, determine who this could be and root out what they desire.

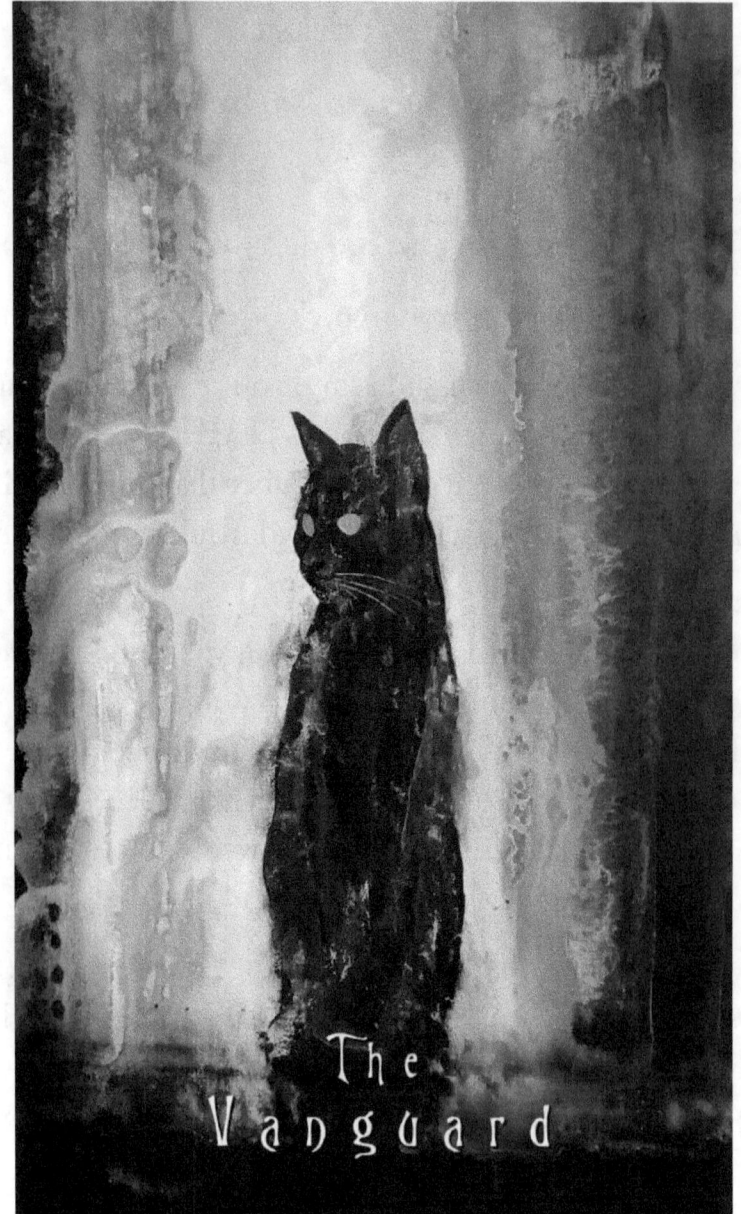

The
Vanguard

The Vanguard

Keywords: Forefront, Independence, New Beginning

When The Vanguard is revealed, it's likely time for you to strike out on your own.

If you've been delaying a big decision involving another person, you should consider taking the lead and making the decision by yourself.

If you've been guilty of procrastination, The Vanguard wants you to immediately get back into motion.

If you're facing doubts about a course of action that have immobilized you, it's time to proceed now or forget the course of action entirely.

The Vanguard wants you to put yourself first. It encourages you to think with a risk/reward state of mind, and if the reward is high, take the plunge. You may have to go at it alone for a while, but others will follow in time.

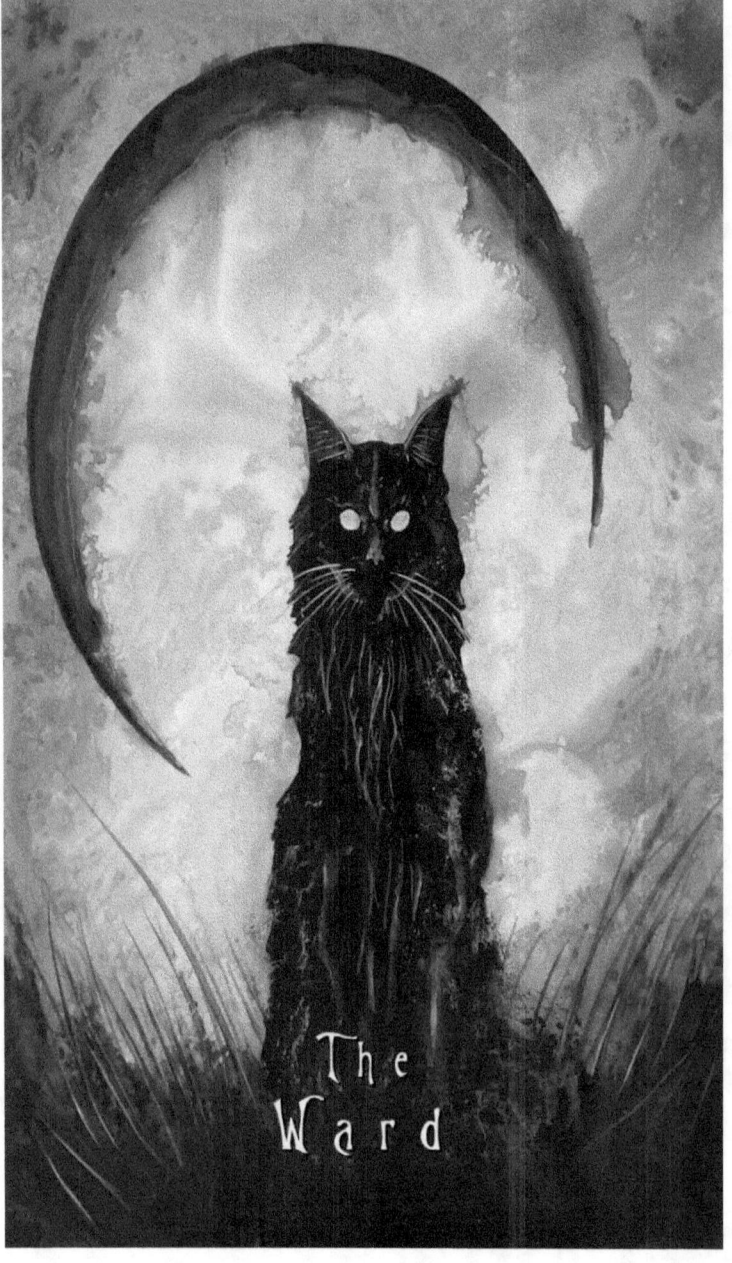

The
Ward

The Ward

Keywords: Shelter, Safety, Home

If you encounter The Ward, it's probable that you or someone close to you needs to retreat to a safe space. This space could be a physical location, such as a new living situation, or a safe emotional state, such as spending extended time with loved ones. This familiar is concerned primarily with building a safe haven for you and your emotions, and with providing you a stable life situation.

Sometimes in life, it's best to stay home, to convalesce, and to begin building a new foundation. With a safe, stable home and a steady support network, you will be capable of much greater feats than if you set out into the world from a position of weakness and instability. The Ward wants you to consider all the volatile and unpredictable elements around you, and to avoid them for the time being.

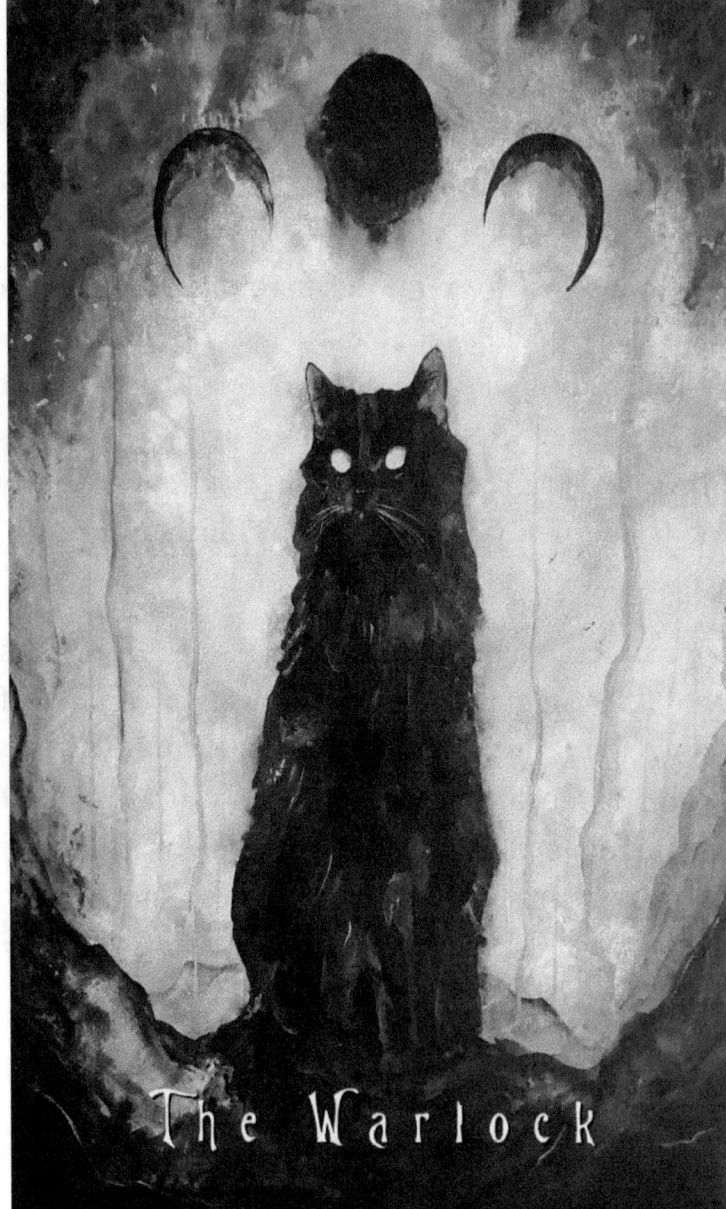

The Warlock

The Warlock

Keywords: Ambition, Charisma, Manifestation

The Warlock wants you to harness your power and to make your dreams come true.

Typically, this familiar will present itself as a strong male figure in your life or as masculine energy harnessed within yourself. In any case, The Warlock is concerned with your advancement, usually either financially or on the social ladder of your life. He desires you to project strength and to move throughout your surroundings with confidence, albeit not arrogance. He wants only the best for you. If you've pulled him, consider your strengths and your personal desires, and take appropriate steps, often loudly and boldly, to attain what you want.

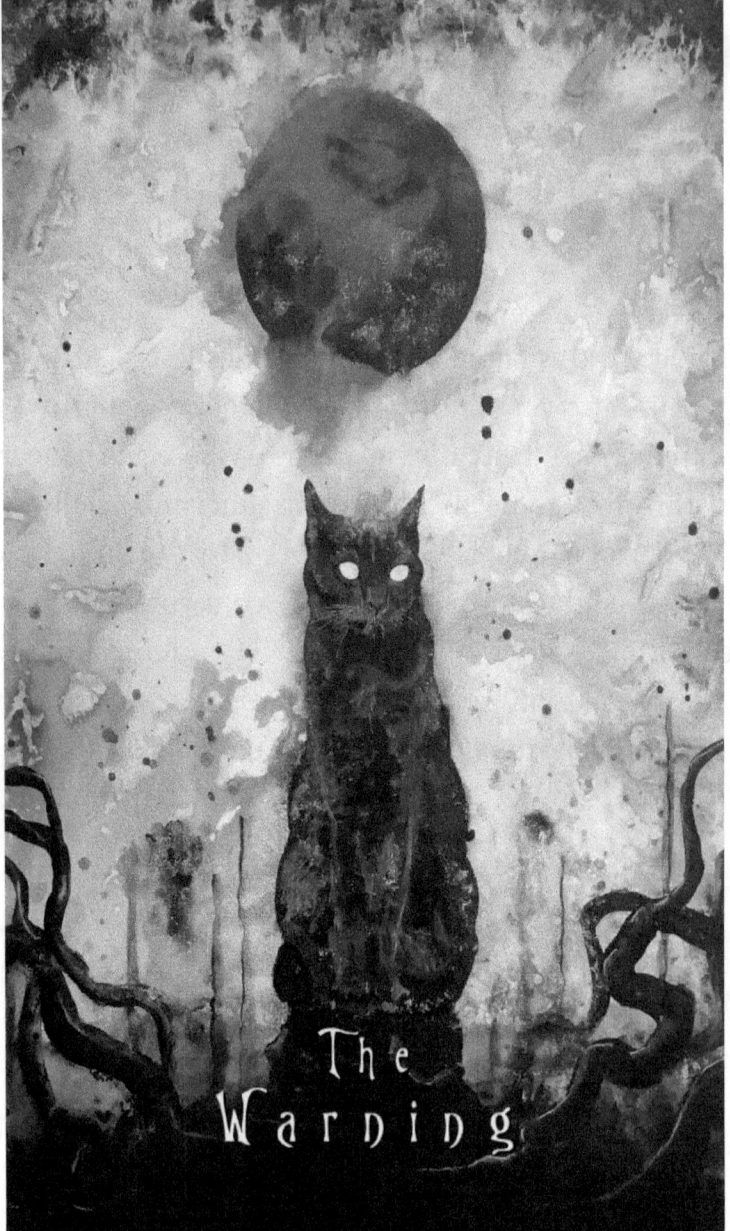

The Warning

Keywords: Alarm, Intimidation, Danger

Someone or something is bringing you trouble.

But this time, there's no backing down.

The Warning is here for a reason you might not expect. She's not here to warn *you*. Rather, she intends to puff up, to raise her hackles, and to frighten away intruders. When she appears, it might be that you're feeling under attack. Someone could be pressuring you to move in an undesirable direction. You might feel the walls of a difficult situation closing in around you.

The Warning won't stand for it, and neither should you.

If you're feeling pressured, walled-in, or bullied, it's time to take a stand. Show the world you mean business. You'll move when you're ready, and only then. This time, you won't bend a knee to anyone or anything.

The Warning reminds us to stand up for ourselves.

Everyday.

Always.

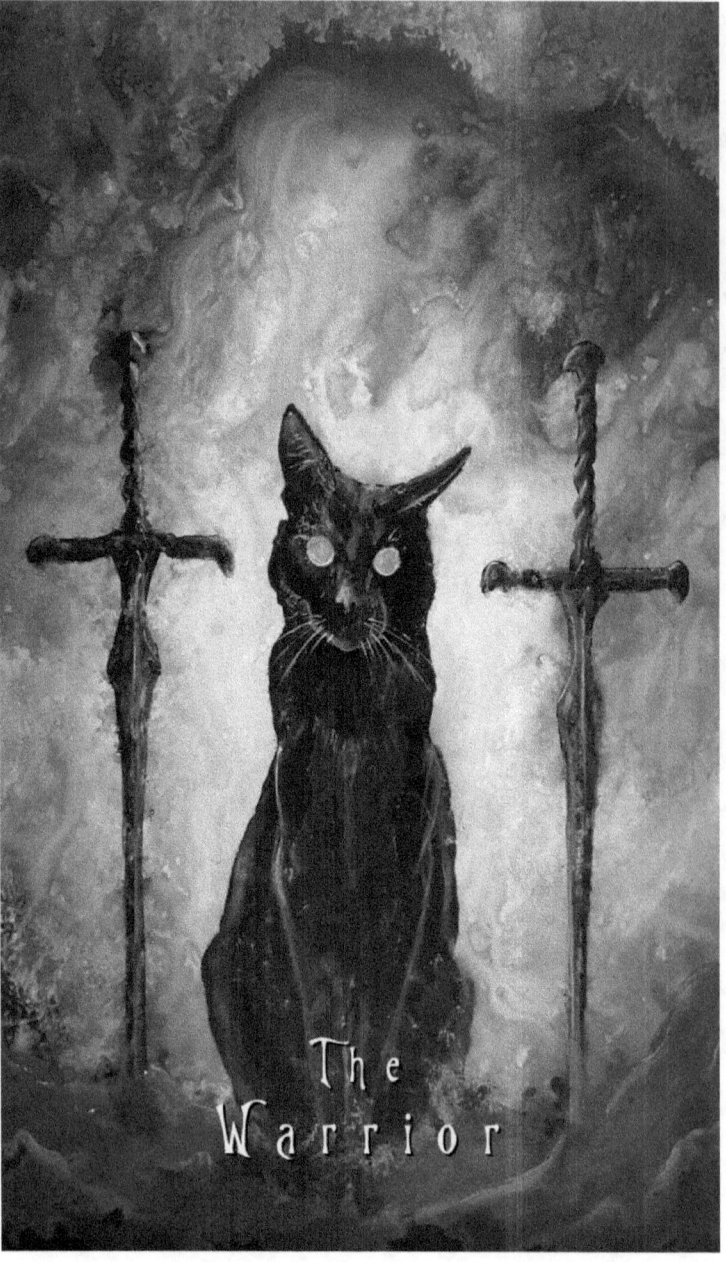

The
Warrior

The Warrior

Keywords: Discipline, Toughness, Resilience

If you've pulled The Warrior, you might think it's time for a fight.

You're only half right.

If this familiar raises its ears in your direction, it's typically because the time is right to tighten the reins on your lifestyle, to cut the excess, and to carve yourself into the very best version of you. If you're feeling lackadaisical or soft of late, it's time to double down on an exercise routine. If you've been showing up late to work or only putting in the bare minimum of effort in some area of your life, it's time to sharpen up and do better.

There's a time and a place for softness. But right now isn't it.

The Warrior reminds us to always strive for self-improvement, even if it's incremental. Do the work to shape yourself into a strong individual, and good things will come.

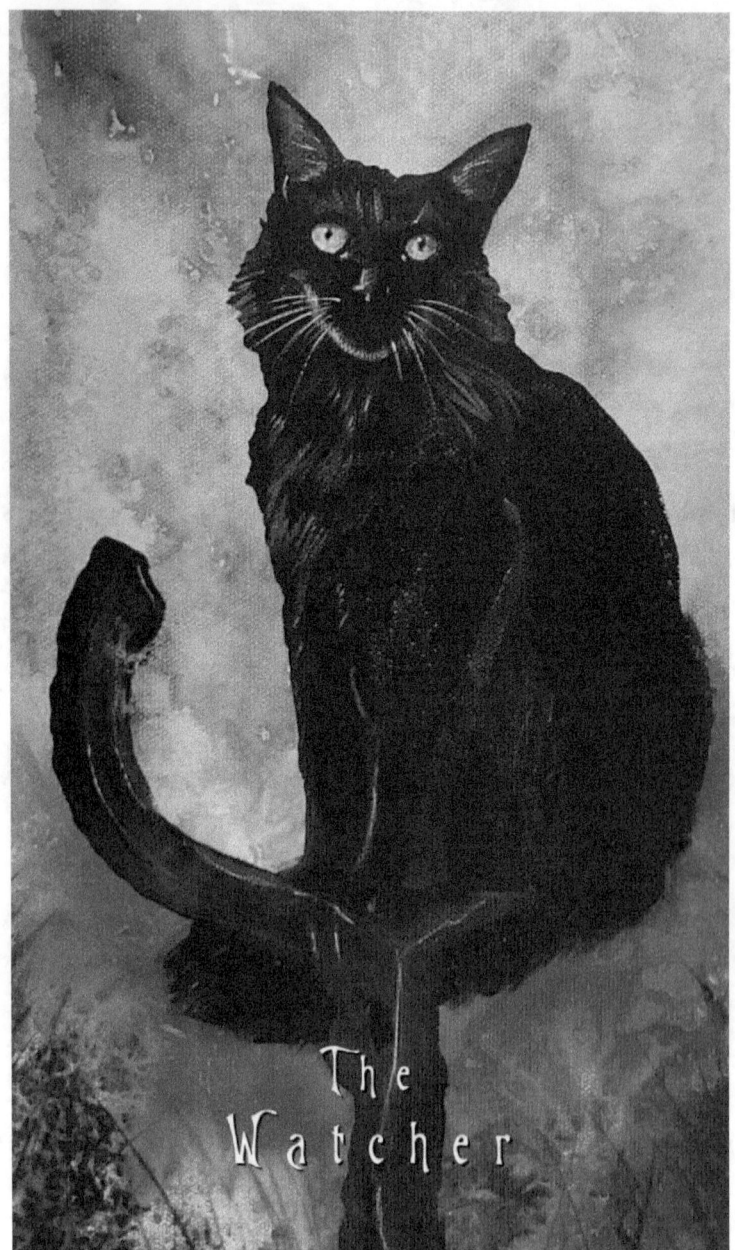

The
Watcher

The Watcher

Keywords: Study, Investigation, Evidence

A learning opportunity is always at hand. This is what The Watcher wants you to remember.

When this familiar arrives, it's time for you to exercise your brain. Read that book you've been putting off. Attend those classes you've been meaning to take. Look deep into your life, open your mind to its fullest, and learn.

If you've been stuck in a particular thought-pattern or resisting the flow of incoming information, now is the time to make a change. We are all students until the end of our days, but only if we allow it. This is your chance to listen to what the other side has to say, to investigate the truth for yourself, to watch and to learn.

The Watcher reminds us to keep our eyes open. Don't assume you already know everything. Consider perspectives and experiences beyond your own. Never stop getting smarter.

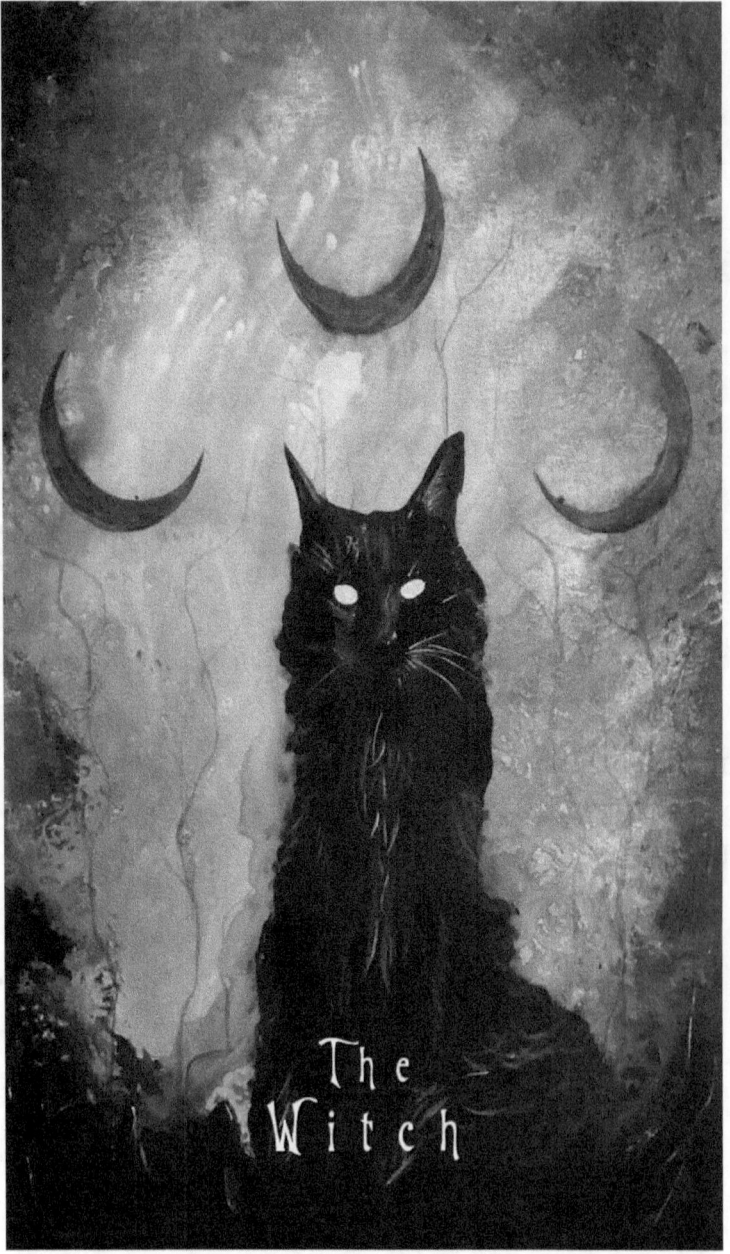

The Witch

Keywords: Creation, Healing, Spirituality

The Witch desires to empower you, to nurture you, and to heal your spiritual wounds.

Typically, this familiar will present itself as a strong female figure in your life or as feminine energy harnessed within yourself. In any case, The Witch is concerned with the health, both physical and emotional, of you and those around you. She desires to shape the world by connecting with nature and with the soulful individual within all people.

If you've pulled her, consider your own spiritual health. Are past emotional injuries taking their toll on you even today? Is there someone close to you in need of uplifting? The Witch believes there is power in all of us to cure the wounds of yesteryear. By attuning with oneself and with the natural world, all things become possible.

More Decks by J Edward Neill

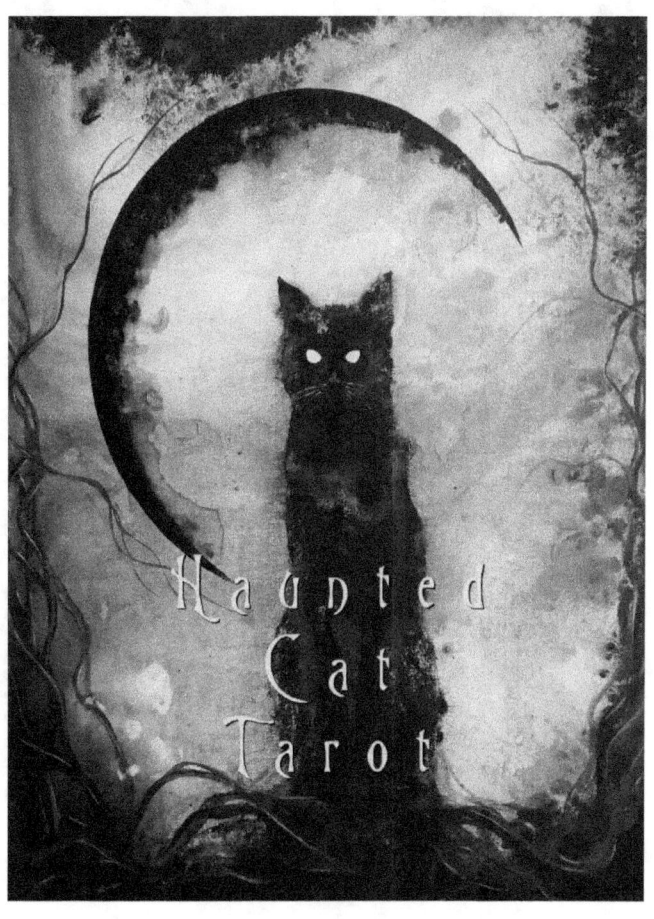

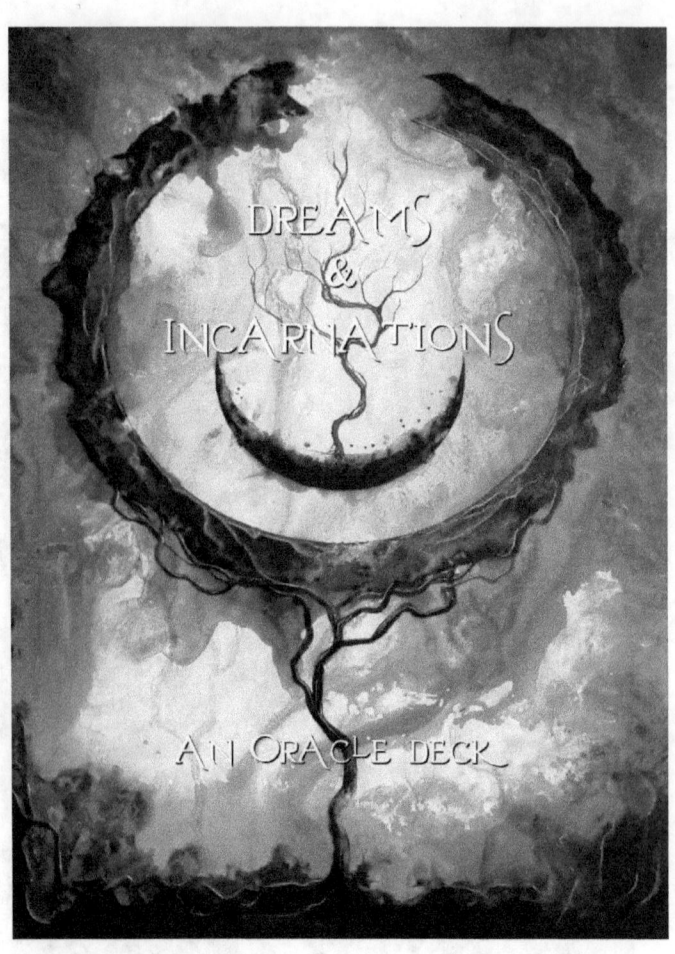

SPIRITS & SHADOWS

AN ORACLE GUIDEBOOK

J EDWARD & HEATHER NEILL

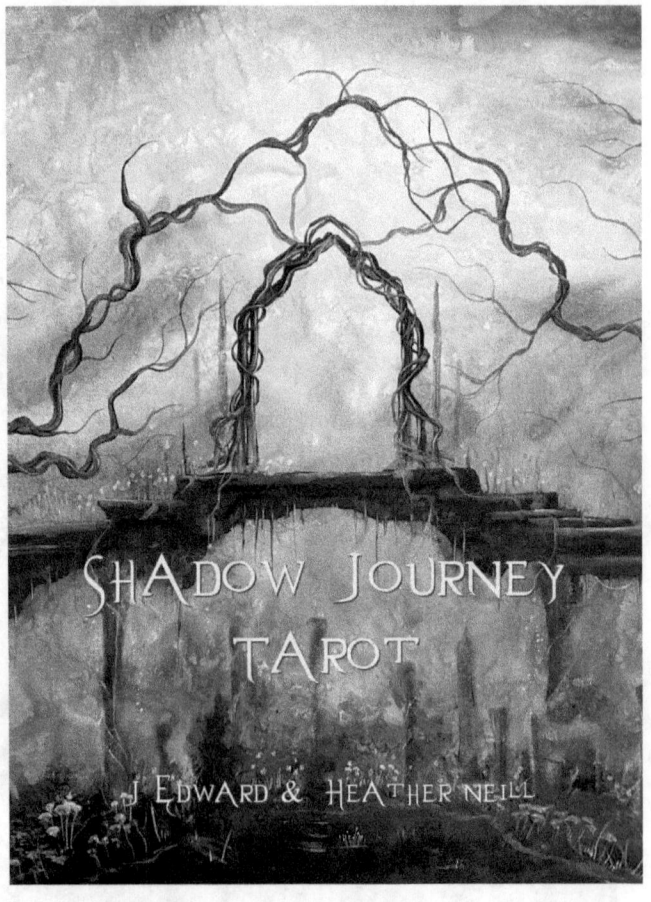

SHADOW JOURNEY TAROT

TAROT

J EDWARD & HEATHER NEILL

About the Author

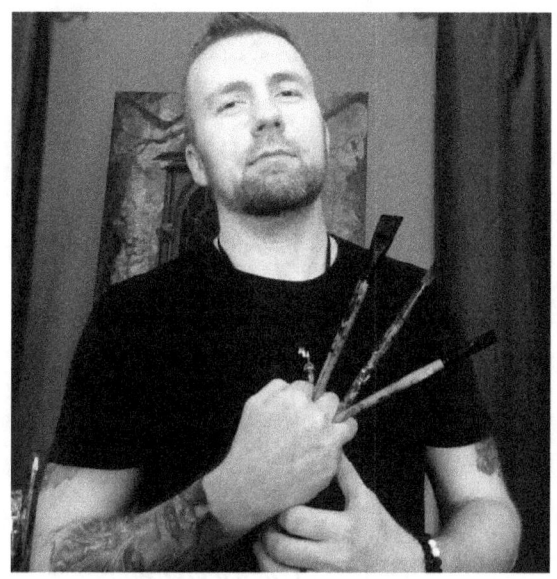

J Edward lives in the volcanic South, writing books, making art, and listening to weird, esoteric music.

Get in touch with his upcoming projects at

ShadowArtFinds.com

Books by J Edward Neill

The Fall of Castle Carrick

Lords of the Black Sands

A Door Never Dreamed Of

The Hecatomb

Hollow Empire – Night of Knives

Eaters of the Light series:

Darkness Between the Stars

Shadow of Forever

Eaters of the Light

Tyrants of the Dead trilogy:

Down the Dark Path

Dark Moon Daughter

Nether Kingdom

Coffee Table Philosophy:

101 Questions for Humanity

444 Questions for the Universe

101 Fun Questions to Ask Your Kids

The Little Book of BIG Questions

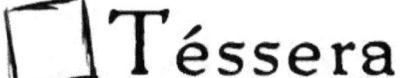
Téssera

www.ingramcontent.com/pod-product-compliance
Lightning Source LLC
Chambersburg PA
CBHW070655220526
45466CB00001B/449